Screen Printing for Quilters

To Gail,

Happy quilting!

Hallie O'Kelley

All photographs by Charles O'Kelley, except where otherwise noted.

Design by Breuna Baine

Cover Photograph by Donahue Studios, Inc., Evansville, Indiana. Courtesy of the American Quilter's Society, Paducah; detail photo by Warren Sams, step-by-step photos by Charlie O'Kelley.

Library of Congress Cataloging-in-Publication Data
O'Kelley, Hallie H., 1924-
      Screen printing for quilters / Hallie H. O'Kelley.
          p.80   cm.8.5"x 11"
      "A Mary Elizabeth Johnson book."
      Includes bibliographical references.
      ISBN 1-881320-44-8 (alk. paper)
      1. Screen process printing. 2. Quilting--Patterns.   I. Title.
TT273. O54   1995
746.6'2--dc20   95-38839
                                                      CIP

Manufactured in the United States of America

Second Printing, April 1996

A MARY ELIZABETH JOHNSON BOOK

 The Black Belt, defined by its dark, rich soil, stretches across central Alabama. It was the heart of the cotton belt. It was and is a place of great beauty, of extreme wealth and grinding poverty, of pain and joy. Here we take our stand, listening to the past, looking to the future.

The Black Belt Press, P.O. Box 551, Montgomery, AL 36101

Contents

Foreword

An exhibition entitled *A Family Affair* showcased the work of four members of a talented family during the summer of 1991 at the Kentuck Museum in Northport, Alabama. On exhibit were photography, jewelry, weaving, and quilts—each format the specialty of one of the family members.

Husband and father Charles O'Kelley brought strong documentary photographs of travels to Mauritius, Alaska, and Kenya. Daughter Celia O'Kelley, M.F.A. candidate at the University of Southern Illinois, presented elegant enamel work in the form of pendants and brooches that were like miniature abstract paintings. Sister Shirley E. Held, retired professor from the College of Design at Iowa State University and author of *Weaving: A Handbook of the Fiber Arts*, showed complex woven portraits of her grandparents.

Mother and sister Hallie O'Kelley exhibited fourteen of her trademark quilts, constructed with her screen printed fabric and stitched with the care of a needlework master. Each quilt was given an appropriate name—*Iowa Summer*, looking like rich farm fields, *Hallie's Comet*, a delightful wordplay on the artist's name and the recurring heavenly visitor, and *Broken Hexagons*, aptly describing a rich geometric design.

The exhibition was wonderful. Each artist had something to say. Each object was thoughtfully conceived, then produced with masterful control of the chosen material. Each statement was complete. But the fact that the individual artists were also tied with family bonds gave an additional dimension to the presentation, one that spoke to a true value of creativity: When it is a part of the fabric of daily life, it emphasizes the importance of the work of the hand for the family and the community.

A greatly simplified history of crafts can be traced from the beginning necessity of making everything by hand for shelter and clothing, through generations of increasingly mechanized production, until handcrafting was nearly gone entirely. However, in the mid-nineteenth century, the protests of the Arts and Crafts Movement over such total industrialization gave birth to a flourishing crafts revival that includes both individual artists and craftsmen, and organized crafts fairs, workshops, and exhibitions.

Hallie O'Kelley and her family are talented examples of the value and function of crafts in today's world. She has increasingly involved crafts in her life, beginning by making objects for personal use to developing a professional career. She started with a master's degree in applied art from Iowa State University in 1950, and went on to enhancing her home environment with objects carefully designed and made by hand. She honed personal skills by attending workshops at such legendary institutions as Arrowmont, and finally, she began entering the arena of juried exhibitions and crafts fairs, where her work is presented to the public, both for viewing and for sale.

Hallie O'Kelley in her booth at The Kentuck Festival of the Arts in Northport, Alabama, with a Merit Award ribbon, one of many she has won in her nine years at the festival.

In her developmental process, Hallie has generously shared her talent with the community. For twelve years, she has designed and printed posters for The Kentuck Festival of the Arts in Northport, Alabama. Her posters always capture exactly the purpose of the event, which is to showcase artists and their work, placing the best statements of contemporary art side by side with the rich examples of Southern tradition. No more perfect motif can be found to illustrate this blending of new and old than the original quilt design Hallie conceives each year.

Hallie O'Kelley's quilts are always magnificent examples of the best of contemporary American crafts. They represent her personal vision and experience. They are thoughtfully designed. They are constructed with absolute control of material and process. She has much to teach—about crafts, about values, about generosity, and about life. Make her lessons a springboard to your own vision.

GEORGINE CLARKE
Visual Arts Program Manager
Alabama State Council on the Arts

5

Dedication

To my husband, Charles, whose help has been invaluable to me. He has drawn patterns, sized diagrams, and photographed all the projects. He has written letters, entered the text into the computer, and has actively sought out avenues for publication. Without his untiring efforts, this book might never have been published, and I am grateful for his tireless support.

Preface

My interest in quilting began as I watched my grandmother quilt in her Iowa home. I learned sewing as a child, and always intended to make a quilt. Through my years in college (I was a home economics major and later a graduate student in applied art with specialization in textile design), I still intended to make a quilt some day. Marriage and four children interrupted the career I had started. For years I made clothes for my family and saved fabric scraps for that quilt I was going to make, eventually accumulating several closet loads of scraps. When my youngest child left home, I decided it was time to start that quilt. In the meantime, I took a refresher course in screen printing and realized how useful this technique can be to a quilter.

At first, I used screen printing primarily as a substitute for appliqué. Then I began to think more in terms of the technique's design possibilities for texture, color, and pattern. Now, I frequently dye fabrics to a color of my choosing before I begin to print on them. I feel a sense of freedom when I can screen-print and dye fabrics to match my mood.

I really love to work with color and also to observe it in nature. Those wonderful intense shades of red in a sunset, and the subtle blue-grays, lavenders, and pinks of the afterglow have inspired me to create quilt designs. A bouquet of zinnias of many hues, all tied together with green, was the beginning of *Zinnias in the Windows of My Log Cabin*.

Since I began designing and making quilts using screen printing (more than 12 years and about 100 quilts ago), I have used some of my long-saved scraps. However, I must confess that most are still in my sewing closet.

History of Screen Printing

Screen printing (known originally as silk-screen printing) is basically a modern-day refinement of the ancient technique of stenciling.

Prehistoric cave dwellers were the first to make and use stencils to produce art, but other primitive cultures also discovered this method for applying decoration. For example, early Fiji Islanders made stencils by cutting perforations in banana leaves; then they applied vegetable dyes through these holes onto bark cloth. (It has been suggested that the natural holes bored or eaten by insects through leaves provided the initial spark of inspiration for this stenciling method.)

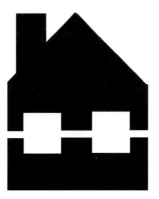

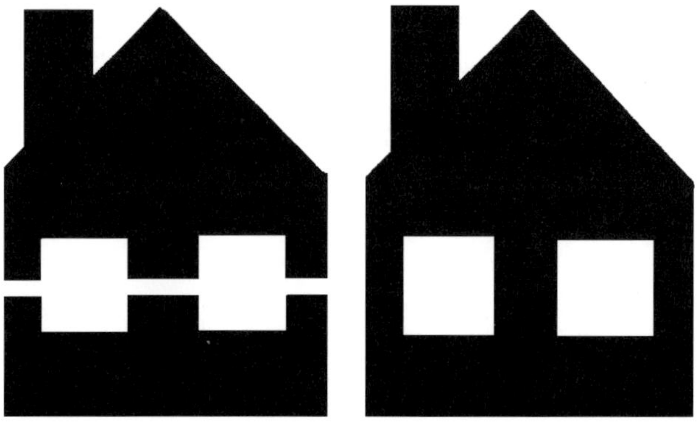

Fig. 1. A stenciled house must use "bridges" to hold the windows (also known as "floating centers") in place.

Fig. 2. A screen printed house can have windows ("floating centers") with no bridges, when the correct material is chosen for the stencil.

For centuries since, artists of many cultures have used small simple stencils in repeating patterns to create complex works of art and for decorating large areas in an all-over design. Paper stencils, dating from perhaps as early as 500 A.D., have been found in the Caves of the Thousand Buddhas in western China. In these stencils, designs were pinpricked on paper and charcoal was rubbed through the pinholes, leaving a pattern of small dots. These dots were then connected with a charcoal pen, and as a final step, color was added.

Ancient Indian, Persian, Egyptian and Roman cultures used stencils in decorating. India and Persia seem to have learned from the Chinese, since they also employed pinpricked stencils. Their contribution was mostly of an aesthetic nature; they refined geometric design to an art.

One drawback to printing with stencils is the difficulty of dealing with "floating centers." For example, if you want to print the figure of a house that has windows, how do you hold the "floating" windows in place while printing? In the ordinary stenciling process, your stencil must contain small "bridges" that connect to the windows and hold that part of your stencil in the correct position (fig.1).

In screen printing the problem of "floating centers" is solved by attaching the entire stencil to a porous screen through which the ink or paint is pressed. There is no need for the connecting "bridges," and the resulting print is aesthetically more pleasing (fig. 2).

Yuensai Miyasaki-Sun, who lived in Japan between 1652 and 1736, is credited with being the first to solve the problem of "floating centers." He held them in place by cementing a network of human hairs from the open center of the design to the rest of the stencil (fig. 3).

The first use of silk as a screen material in Europe appears to have been in France about 1870. Because silk was also the base fabric to which the design was applied, the resulting printed fabrics were quite costly and found only a limited market. However, the printing method nonetheless spread from France to Switzerland and other European countries. In 1907, nearly forty years after its introduction, the fabric-printing process that used stencils adhered to porous silk screens was patented by Samuel Simon of Manchester, England.

Printing through the stenciled silk was initially done using a stiff brush to push the ink through the porous fabric. Later the squeegee replaced the brush, speeding up and improving the process. The squeegee is a rubber blade held in a wooden handle. The printer pulls it across the silk screen, which presses the ink in a uniform layer onto the paper or fabric to which the design is being applied.

Using squeegees for commercial printing on paper developed rapidly thereafter, in both Europe and the United States. In 1922, the Naz-Dar Company was founded in Chicago to manufacture inks specifically for screen printing. The first inks developed became quite stiff when dry, giving fabrics an undesirable hand. Because of this, screen printing on fabric developed slowly. Beginning in the 1950s, however, inks began to be manufactured that left the printed fabric quite flexible and easily draped.

Even with the marvelous technological advances made in paints and inks, very little work in the medium of screen printing on fabric has been exhibited in art shows. Even today, only a few quilters make use of this versatile technique. I hope my book will change this and that more people will come to enjoy the technique I have learned to love.

Fig. 3. In this old Japanese stencil, a network of crossed hairs is used to hold "floating centers" in place.

9

Getting Ready To Print

Screen printing is not expensive, nor does it require extensive or complicated equipment. Much of what you need can be made at home from inexpensive materials easily available at discount and/or art supply stores. Any specialized materials can be mail-ordered (sources are given on page 79). If you are new to this wonderful way of creating your own designs, you need to familiarize yourself with the supplies required, which are listed below. Also following is detailed information on those items that are specific to the craft.

Print cloth
Screen material
Wooden printing frame
Stencil material
Stencil cutting knife and circle cutter
Adhering liquid
Printing ink (paint)
Printing board
Squeegee
T-pins
Blow-dryer

Print Cloth

This is the fabric that will be printed with your design. Cotton print cloth, mercerized or not, can be purchased from suppliers such as Testfabrics, Inc. or Dharma Trading Co. It is reasonably priced. Most print cloth available is 44-45" wide.

Bleached or unbleached muslin, generally available in fabric stores, may also be suitable; just be sure to thoroughly wash it before use to remove all sizing.

Any cloth with a permanent finish, such as crease-resistance, drip-dry and permanent press, can be used; however, the printing ink is more likely to bleed beyond the margins of the stencil before the ink is dry. Also, the ink may not adhere as well as it does to a fabric without a finish.

Screen Material

The first quality to consider when choosing a fabric for a screen material is that it should be porous enough to allow the printing ink through, but not so loosely constructed that it allows the ink to run. Possibilities include polyester, silk, nylon, and cotton organdy. Art-supply stores and screen-printing supply houses commonly carry all of these materials except organdy, but it can be found in fabric shops.

Polyester is used most often and it is what I recommend for printing on fabric. Its only disadvantage is that some photographic stencils do not adhere as well to polyester as to natural silk. However, polyester is preferable to natural silk because it does not change shape with variations in temperature and humidity. It is also less expensive. Nylon, like silk, reacts to temperature changes; it also tends to stretch with use. If you must use nylon, wet it before stretching it on the frame. Organdy is the least suitable because it has a tendency to stretch.

The coarseness or fineness of a screen fabric is described by its mesh number. For printing on cloth I recommend using a multifilament polyester screen fabric with a 12XX designation.

Printing Frames

The screen material will be stretched on a frame. Although you can buy frames from an art-supply house at moderate cost, it's easy and inexpensive to make them yourself. For small frames, use 1 x 1-inch softwood finished strips (sand them if necessary). If you have a miter box, miter the corners (fig.4); if not, saw the strip ends square and abut them when you put the four pieces together (fig.5). Glue the ends together temporarily with water-soluble glue, then secure with tacks or small nails. The screen material will be attached to the sides of the finished frame, so the sides are flat. For 2 x 2-foot or larger frames, use 2 x 2-inch softwood strips, and attach angle irons at the corners to give the frame greater rigidity (fig.6).

I recommend painting finished frames with oil-base paint because you will wash the stencil, screen and frame with water after you use them.

A somewhat more expensive alternative is to use canvas stretching frames, available from art supply houses. While these may not be quite as sturdy as permanent frames, they are an advantage if you are not an experienced carpenter. Also, after removing the screen material, they can be taken apart and stored in less space than a permanent frame will require.

Stretching the Screen Fabric on the Printing Frame

One of my teachers said that a properly stretched screen will bounce a cat, letting us know that our goal was to have our screen material pulled tautly across the wooden frame and stapled securely.

Stapling the screen to the frame can be done by one person, but it is easier as a two-person operation, particularly if the printing frame is large. One person pulls the fabric tight while the other operates a carpenter's staple gun.

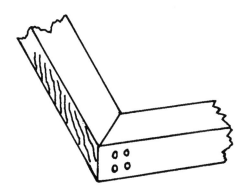

Fig 4. Wooden frame with mitered edges.

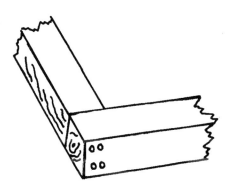

Fig. 5. Wooden frame corner with square strip ends.

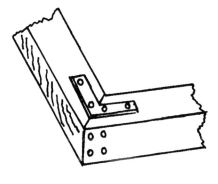

Fig. 6. Wooden frame corner reinforced with angle irons.

11

Cut a piece of your screen material so that it extends 1 1/2 inches on all sides of your frame. Using the staple gun, staple the center of one side of the fabric to the corresponding side of the frame. Since the fabric is larger than the frame, this staple and all others can be placed into the side, rather than the face, of the frame. While pulling a corner of the fabric tight, staple along this side of the frame, working outward from the center. Place a staple about every inch as you move outward. Do the same thing on the other side of the central staple (fig. 7).

Repeat this process on the opposite side of the frame. Then go to either of the other sides; pull the fabric tight and staple in a similar manner, from the center to the corners. Finally, repeat the process on the fourth side of the frame.

It is most important to stretch the fabric tight, like a drumhead, over the face of the frame. You may use a pair of fabric pliers to pull the screen material tight.

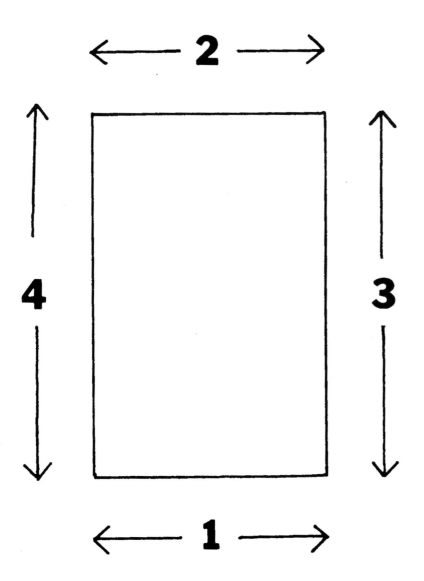

Fig. 7. Diagram for stretching and stapling the screen fabric to the frame. Begin in the center of Side 1 and work from the center to both ends. Repeat for Side 2, then Side 3 and Side 4.

Stencil Material

There are several different types of material used for making stencils. Read about all of them, then choose the type that will suit your project. The directions for the individual projects in this book tell you which type of stencil material is best for each, but you will soon learn to judge for yourself.

Special tools you'll find helpful when cutting stencils are a stencil-cutting knife, such as X-Acto, and a circle cutter. Both are available at larger art-supply stores.

Simple Paper or Plastic Stencils: Paper and clear plastic are the least expensive materials appropriate for stencils. They work especially well for figures or silhouetted designs. Let's assume you are making a crib quilt and wish to decorate the sashing with repeated

larger than the printing frame and cutting the heart outline into the plastic. The plastic square becomes the stencil.

A good feature of these unmounted stencils is that you can roll them up and store them in a small space for future use.

Cut-Lacquer Stencils: The stencil material known as cut-lacquer film is preferred when the design you wish to print features fine detail. It is particularly useful in preparing stencils with "floating centers" described on page 8.

Cut-lacquer film, also known as knife-cut film, comes in double-layered sheets. A thin, translucent lacquer layer, ordinarily green or amber colored, adheres to a thicker, transparent polyvinyl backing. You can get this film at art-supply stores or screen-print-

Fig. 8. Place the frame screen side down on the cut lacquer stencil and rub the adhering liquid through the screen.

Fig. 9. A finished cut-lacquer stencil from the top side.

hearts. On a piece of paper slightly larger than your printing frame (tracing paper or a similar thin paper with a hard finish works best), draw a heart. Place the drawing on cardboard; then use a sharp knife, such as the X-Acto, or razor blade to cut through the paper along the outline of the heart. Your tracing paper is now a simple stencil.

You can make a more durable simple stencil by first drawing the heart on paper, then overlaying it with a square of clear polyethylene sheeting (3 mil weight) slightly

ing supply houses.

To make a stencil using this material, place the film, lacquer side up, over a drawing of the stencil you wish to prepare. The dimensions of the film should be slightly smaller than the inner dimensions of your screen frame. Using a sharp knife, cut the design through the lacquer layer only. When you finish cutting, carefully peel off the cut areas of the lacquer layer, leaving a "hole" through which the printing ink will pass. Start the peeling with the point of your sten-

13

cil knife, a pin or a needle.

You will adhere the stencil (after peeling) to the screen using an organic solvent called adhering liquid. *Avoid contact with the adhering liquid; use rubber gloves and work in a well-ventilated area.* Place the stencil, lacquer side up, on a smooth surface (such as glass). Position a screen-covered print frame over it, placing the screen side down. Dampen a small cloth or piece of cotton with adhering liquid and rub it over the screen fabric, pressing gently. Immediately afterward, rub the screen fabric with a dry cloth to take up any excess solvent. The stencil is adhered to the screen when the solvent completely evaporates. Finally, peel away the polyvinyl backing from the adhered lacquer stencil (fig. 8).

Before you begin to print, use masking tape to seal all stencil edges to the wooden frame. Any gaps may be closed by taping transparent plastic strips bottom side of the screen and frame (fig.9).

Cut-lacquer film is more expensive than plastic sheeting, but you can make hundreds of prints before it wears out. When you no longer need the stencil, remove it from the screen with lacquer thinner.

Contact Paper Stencils: Contact Paper is the trade name for a self-adhering vinyl sheet with a paper backing, and it is widely available in department and discount stores. Since pressure is all that is needed to make this material adhere directly to the screen material on your printing frame, it allows you to affix a stencil quickly and simply. To make this kind of stencil, choose the translucent variety of Contact Paper, and draw a mirror image of your design on the paper backing. Cut the stencil, using a knife or scissors. Remove the paper backing, and press the sticky side of the clear film to the bottom side of the screen and frame.

Photographic Stencils: A photographic stencil is the ultimate material for stencils,

better than cut-lacquer for capturing fine detail. If you want to include a detailed drawing or a portrait of Great-Uncle Charlie in your family-history quilt, this is the stencil to use. As the name implies, a photographic stencil is a means of transferring actual photographs onto fabric. Although the process might sound somewhat daunting as you read about it, it is actually not so difficult at all, and working with photographs can be quite a bit of fun. A bathroom can be temporarily converted to a darkroom for developing the photographic stencil. Once you try it, you will be fascinated with the possibilities.

Start with a really good black-and-white photograph, one that is clear and focused, not fuzzy or damaged. Unless you have a lot of skill and a well-equipped photographic laboratory, I suggest that you take your photograph to a professional and ask him to make a positive transparency in the size you wish your finished print to be. If your photograph has gray areas in it (your photo of Great-Uncle Charlie will certainly have these) specify that the positive transparency should be a 65-line halftone (or something close to that). You will use this transparency as your starting image.

Photographic stencil material is available in several types in sheets or on rolls. I recommend indirect photographic stencil material, which has an emulsion layer coated onto a plastic support sheet. The emulsion layer is comparable to any photographic film, because it is sensitive to light, in this case, blue and ultraviolet but not yellow or red. Therefore, the sheets of stencil material can be handled and processed under a yellow or red safelight or even under subdued incandescent light.

To make the printing stencil, place the indirect photographic stencil sheet down, emulsion side up; then cover this with the positive transparency emulsion side down.

Cover both with a piece of plate glass to ensure good contact between the transparency and the stencil sheet. Expose the stencil sheet to a bright light of even intensity. Areas that are struck by light are hardened, while unexposed areas (such as those under Uncle Charlie's black beard) remain soft. (About all I can say about exposure time is to go by trial and error.)

When the exposure to light is completed, the image must be developed like an ordinary piece of photographic film, under a safelight or subdued incandescent light. Chemicals and instructions for development will be supplied with the particular brand of photographic stencil material you use. When the development is complete, you will wash the stencil sheet with a stream of warm water. The soft, unexposed emulsion washes away, while the hardened exposed emulsion remains in place on the plastic support sheet.

The final step is the pressing of the stencil sheet, emulsion side down, against the printing screen, which has been stretched on a regular printing frame. When the emulsion is completely dry, pull away the plastic support sheet. The stencil is now ready for printing.

I should caution you that photographic stencils are water soluble to some extent. They will wear away as you print if you are using water-soluble ink. Therefore, a limited number of prints of Great-Uncle Charlie can be produced before the edges of the stencil wear and the prints become fuzzy. If you need a number of prints of Uncle Charlie, go ahead and make several stencils at once.

Printing Inks

Inks (occasionally referred to as paints) suitable for screen printing on fabric have specific properties. They must be thin enough to pass through the pores of the screen but thick enough to produce a clear image on the print cloth. (They are actually gel-like in texture.) Inks should dry relatively quickly but not so rapidly that the screen's pores clog while you are printing. Finally, they must adhere well to the print cloth and not bleed before they dry. Good commercially prepared fabric-printing inks have these properties.

I recommend that quilters work with water-base inks. When you finish printing, you can clean your squeegee, stencils, and screens with tap water. Most cleanup tasks can be accomplished in the kitchen sink; clean larger items outside using a hose.

Suitable water-soluble printing inks in a variety of colors can be purchased from Dharma Trading Co. (Deka Permanent Fabric Paint and Versatex Textile Paint), Hunt-Speedball (Textile Inks-Heat Set), The Naz-Dar Company (WAT-R-TEX), Craft Industries Limited (PROfab Textile Ink and Pebeo Setacolor Transparent), and PRO Chemical and Dye, Inc.(PROfab Textile Ink). Extender base (added to lighten colors without thinning the ink) is available for these inks from each of the companies. Refer to page 79 for a list of ink suppliers and their addresses.

If you wish to prepare large quantities of ink more economically, Sax Arts and Crafts provides a variety of Colortex Textile Pigments that you add to an extender called Colortex Base. This is a concentrated base to which a measured amount of water is added before use. As a final step, you add pigment to the white diluted base to give the desired color and tint.

All inks in the preceding discussion are translucent. If you prefer, you may work with opaque fabric inks, available from Union.

Printing inks are reasonably stable and can be stored indefinitely under refrigeration in a frost-free refrigerator. The container should be sealed to prevent inks from drying out.

Print Boards

A print board is the cushioned surface on which you print the fabric. I find that a board measuring 24 inches square and made of 1/2-inch thick plywood is most useful for printing small pieces of fabric. My largest board was made using a 48-inch square of 1/2 inch plywood. (Do not assume that print boards must be square; they should be shaped to easily accommodate your design.)

Print boards are easy to make. Cover one side of your plywood shape with 1/2- to 3/4-inch-thick foam, such as upholstery or carpet padding, wrapping it around all sides to the back. (Your local carpet dealer may have scraps he will give you. Even if it isn't free, the small piece you need won't cost much.) The padding may be glued to the wood, but this is not usually necessary. Stretch unbleached muslin or an old sheet over the padding, and staple it to the back of the board.

An alternative to plywood is wallboard, which weighs less. The padding and fabric cover should be taped, rather than stapled, to the back of the wall board.

The Squeegee

The squeegee, as mentioned before, is used to push ink through the screen onto the print cloth underneath. The type most commonly used consists of a rubber or polyurethane strip about 1/4 inch thick by 2 inches wide by whatever length is needed for printing. The strip is held tightly in a wooden handle with about 1 inch of the rubber (or polyurethane) blade extending downward (fig. 10).

The squeegee should be at least an inch longer than the width of the design to be printed. On the other hand, the strip and handle should be slightly shorter than the inside width of your printing frame. Screen-printing supply houses will make this type of squeegee to your specified length. Other pieces of plastic with a smooth edge, such as an old credit card can be used as a squeegee. One of my favorite small squeegees is a plastic plate-scraper.

Fig. 10. Rubber squeegee with wooden handle.

Twelve Projects You Can Make

Screen printing adds another dimension to your possibilities as a quiltmaker. It should be regarded as an addition to the skills you presently possess, not as a substitute for any of them. You may want to screen-print the blocks of a baby quilt, then piece the sashing and borders. You may appliqué the blocks for a floral quilt and screen-print the borders. Or you may devise projects that incorporate all three of these quilt-making techniques, plus others such as embroidery. There is no limit.

To get you started in the technique and to help you gain confidence with it, I am sharing with you twelve of my original quilt designs, each especially chosen for the techniques you will experience. The projects are arranged in order according to the amount of skill required to complete each quilt. A *Cat-and-Mouse Game* is the simplest of all the designs, and *Zinnias in the Window of My Log Cabin* is the most complex (although not beyond your reach once you know how to screen-print). I have made all of these quilts myself, many of them more than one time, and I think you will enjoy each design as much as I have. At the end of the projects, a gallery of other quilts I have made is presented to show you what is possible.

A Cat-and-Mouse Game is a miniature quilt involving only three small stencils. I have designed a number of miniatures that include animal figures, and this one seems to be almost everyone's favorite.

Broken Hexagons is a wall quilt that involves a single stencil. It hangs on a white wall in the entrance to my more-or-less contemporary-style home. It is my husband's favorite; he says it has elegant simplicity.

Phil O'Dendron is the easiest full-sized quilt in the book. Does my last name tell you what inspired me to design this green quilt?

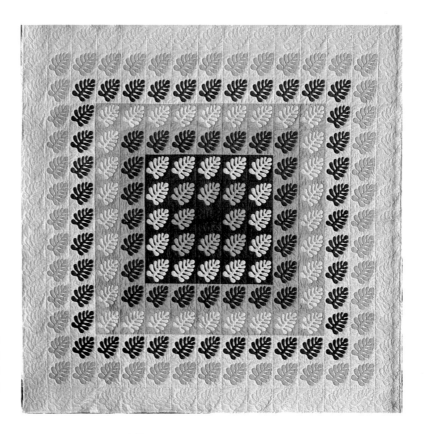

Paper Dolls is an easy-to-make crib quilt that employs silhouette stencils. Part of the stencils must be cut freehand, which is only a little harder than cutting straight lines. The quilt can be printed using any two colors you choose. The quilts I have made from this design have been very popular, both with friends and festival customers.

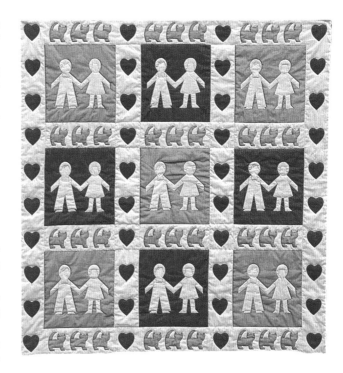

Festival Tree was inspired by the logo of the Kentuck Festival of the Arts, where I frequently exhibit and sometimes win prizes. It is unique among these twelve quilts presented here in that it uses a "spot of color" printing technique that I originated. I will tell you how to add a "spot of color" to the background of your quilts in the instructions.

Counterpoint is a wall quilt whose design is geometric and involves overlapping printing. The critical lesson you will learn in making this design is how to handle a stencil when positioning.

Which Came First? My daughter, an enamalist-artist, and I designed this quilt together. It involves printing several colors adjacent to one another, which requires a bit of advanced skill. It so charmed the editors of *McCall's Quilting* that they made it the feature of an article in the magazine (although they gave directions for appliqué rather than screen-printing).

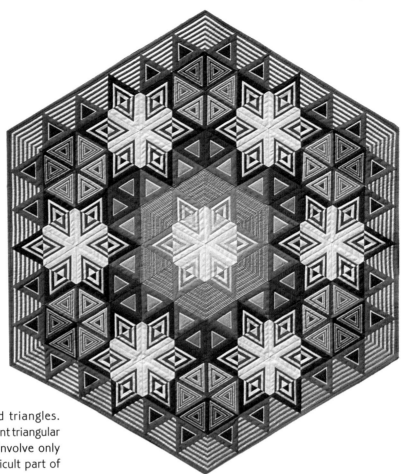

Hexad is made of pieced triangles. Although a number of different triangular stencils must be cut, they involve only straight lines. The most difficult part of making this quilt is piecing the triangles together. This quilt is a good one to hang over the headboard of a bed.

Reach Out and Touch Someone combines screen printing with appliqué, which is used for the embellishing touches. The hands represent the five races of humankind that must strive to live together in harmony.

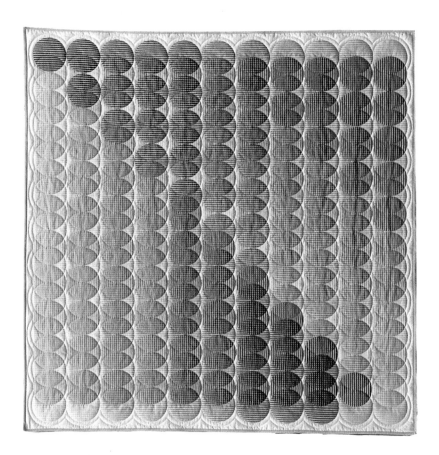

After the Sunset is similar to *Counterpoint*, but more complex in its design and therefore a little more difficult to print. The stencils used to make this quilt allow you numerous variations within the basic design, depending on how you arrange colors. I have included another version in the Gallery Section, beginning on page 74.

Grandpa's Farm was inspired by the Iowa farm where I lived as a child. It is another of my most popular designs.

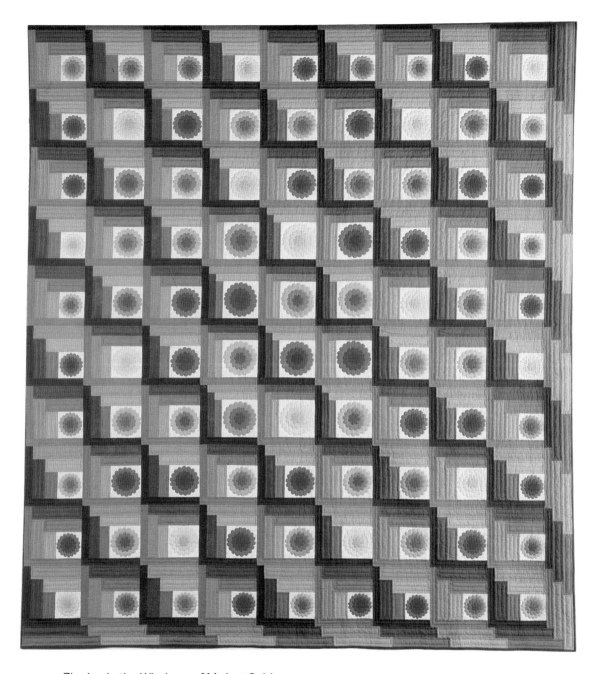

Zinnias in the Windows of My Log Cabin was designed and made for exhibit in the Theme Class of the 1987 American Quiilter's Society show. The original is now in the permanent collection of the Society's museum. (Photography by Donahue Studios, Inc., Evansville, Indiana. Courtesy of the American Quilter's Society, Paducah, Kentucky.)

Let the Printing Begin

By the time you are ready to print, you have done most of the work. Now the fun begins. You will need to think ahead to plan where you are going to dry all your newly-printed motifs, because you can make them so fast you could run out of drying room in a hurry.

You are ready to print when:

1. You have worked out your colors;
2. Your stencils are cut (always remember that you need a stencil for each color, unless you plan to repeat the same motif in a different color);
3. Your printing frame is ready and your screen is stretched;
4. You have cut your print cloth into the sizes needed for the project you are making.

Position the print cloth, right side up, on the print board and smooth it flat. Stretch the cloth firmly across the surface of the print board, and hold it in place by pinning the

edges of the cloth with T-pins; angle them toward the center of the board as you insert them into the padding.

(*Tip:* Positioning guides help insure proper placement of the stencil. Stretch and pin black threads on top of the print cloth so that the surface of the print board is divided into equal-size blocks. In the photographs at right, you will see that my board is divided into thirds horizontally and vertically, making nine equal-size blocks.)

Carefully place the stencil in the proper position on the stretched print cloth. When you are satisfied that it is correctly positioned, place your printing frame on top of the stencil (fig. 11). Apply the printing ink inside the frame to one side of the stencil (use a generous amount, as shown in fig. 12). Hold the frame securely; then place a squeegee inside the frame to the outside of the ink (fig. 13), and draw it across the screen to the other side of the frame. Use moderate pressure; repeat passes of the squeegee two to four times to give an even, clean print; add extra ink if needed. A test print can help you determine how much ink and how many passes are needed.

Lift the stencil and frame straight up from the completed print (fig.14). Sliding them sideways may cause smearing. When you lift up the screen, you will find that the stencil has attached itself to the bottom of the screen. You do not need to separate the two to make additional prints. As you finish each print, set it aside to dry.

(*Tip:* Inks sometime have a tendency to bleed (spread slightly beyond the printed

24

Fig. 11. Printing frame on top of a paper stencil, which has been positioned carefully onto the right side of the print. cloth.

Fig. 12. Ink ready for use inside printing frame.

Fig. 13. Squeegee in place prior to printing.

Fig. 14. Finished print.

edge) before they dry. To prevent this, use a blow-dryer (the kind you use for your hair) to quickly dry your print. Only when your print is dry can you add another color.)

Positioning a second stencil is critical, but simple. Just look down through the second stencil at your initial print. When the second stencil is properly placed, put the print screen for that stencil over it, add the correct color ink, and you are ready to print. Dry the second color thoroughly before adding another; each color must be completely and thoroughly dry before you screen another color onto the design.

Note: If you are using a cut-lacquer stencil (which is adhered to the screen before printing), the basic printing procedure is the same as for the loose, unmounted stencil just described.

Heat Setting

After all the colors are printed and thoroughly dry, the ink must be heat-set for color fastness. Place your prints in a baking pan, cover with foil, and bake for 5 minutes in a 300-degree oven. The manufacturer of your inks may suggest other ways to heat-set them.

Correcting Printing Problems

Although the process of screen-printing is not at all complicated, some practice sessions will help you identify the problems that can occur and you can learn how to correct them before you move on to your final project. I have identified the most common mistakes my students make and the ways to avoid them.

Too Much Ink on Printed Image

Cause: Too many passes of the squeegee.

Solutions: Use only two passes of squeegee or
Hold squeegee more upright (45- to 60-degree angle between squeegee and board) so that it clears the stencil of ink as it travels across.

Image Is Smeared

Cause: The screen slipped.

Solutions: After printing, lift print frame up carefully or
Find a helper to hold the frame while you print or
Don't apply so much pressure to the squeegee.

Ink Bleeds

Causes: Wrong kind of fabric or
Not drying quick enough after printing.

Solutions: Test fabric before printing and
Use a blow-dryer.

Uneven Covering of Ink

Causes: Not enough ink on screen when you began to squeegee or
Not enough passes with the squeegee or
Squeegee is too small to cover stencil image or
Screen is clogged.

Solutions: Start with more ink or
Make more passes with the squeegee or
Use a larger squeegee or
Wash and dry screen; then print more quickly.

Small White Flecks in Printed Image

Cause: Debris on screen before you print.

Solutions: Brush screen before you apply any ink and/or
Wash and dry screen and start printing again.

Streaked Color

Cause: Ink not mixed thoroughly before it is used.

Solution: Stir ink thoroughly before printing.

Mixing Colors

Prepared inks and pigments come in a wide variety of colors, but you will also want to know how to mix inks or pigments to make your own colors. This keeps you from being limited to the colors you can buy. It is easier to mix correctly if you know something about color fundamentals.

Color experts frequently describe colors as being primary, secondary, or tertiary. Primary colors include blue, red, and yellow (fig. 15). Equal amounts of two primaries result in a secondary color; for example, blue and red make violet, red and yellow make orange, blue and yellow make green. A mixture of equal amounts of each of the three primaries produces black. Tertiary colors are obtained by mixing primary colors in unequal proportions.

In mixing pigments or inks for printing, factors other than color must be considered. Once you have obtained the desired color, you may wish to lighten (tint) it by adding extender or opaque white. If you wish to darken (shade) the color, add black. Finally, you can decrease the intensity (tone) of the color by adding gray or some of the complementary color.

Other relationships of different colors may be described in terms of a twelve-color wheel (fig. 16). On this color wheel, complementary colors are opposite each other in

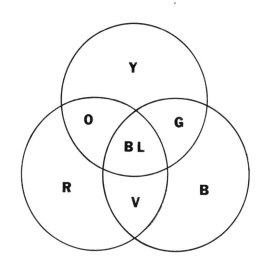

Fig. 15. A twelve-color wheel. R–red, RO–red-orange, O–orange, YO–yellow-orange, Y–yellow, YG–yellow-green, G–green, BG–blue-green, B–blue, BV–blue-violet, V–violet, RV–red-violet.

the circle. Mixing two complementary colors, or pigments, together in equal proportions produces gray. Color mixing should always be done under natural light, preferably coming through a north window. Artificial light changes colors in inconsistent ways, making it difficult to match colors.

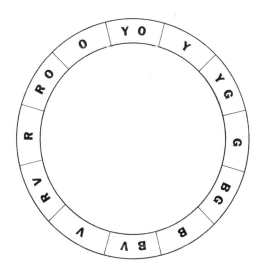

Fig. 16. The relationship of primary colors (Y–yellow, R–red, B–blue) to secondary colors (O–orange, V–violet, G–green) and to black (BL).

A CAT-AND-MOUSE GAME

A miniature or doll quilt

(overall size: 11 1/4 x 11 3/4 inches)

This adorable quilt is a snap to print and easy to construct. Only three easy-to-cut stencils are needed. Because the figures are mere silhouettes, you have the choice of either paper or plastic stencils. This is a simple little design, so if you have a misprint you can easily replace this with little expense of time or money. (*Note:* Because it is a miniature, *all seams are 1/8 inch*, rather than the regular 1/4-inch seams used in the larger quilts described elsewhere.)

Stencils Required

1. Background around cat
2. Background around mouse
3. Mouse

Ink Colors

1. Dark blue for background
2. Pink for mouse

Fabric and Special Thread Required

1. Print cloth: one 3 1/2- x 45-inch strip (cut long side on the selvage) and one piece 13 inches square for backing.
2. Dark-blue solid fabric: two pieces 1 x 27 inches cut crosswise for the binding.
3. Medium-blue solid fabric: one piece 5 1/2-x 12 inches.
4. Light-blue solid fabric: one piece 5 1/2- x12 inches.
5. Black quilting thread for the cat's whiskers.
6. Pink embroidery floss for the mouse tail.

Cutting Instructions

1. From the 45-inch strip of print cloth, cut twelve 3 1/2-x 2 1/2-inch rectangles.
2. From the light-blue fabric, cut one 1 x 11 3/4-inch strip for the left border the quilt and twelve of pattern piece C.
3. From the medium-blue fabric, cut one 1 x 10 1/4-inch strip for the bottom quilt border and twelve of pattern piece D.

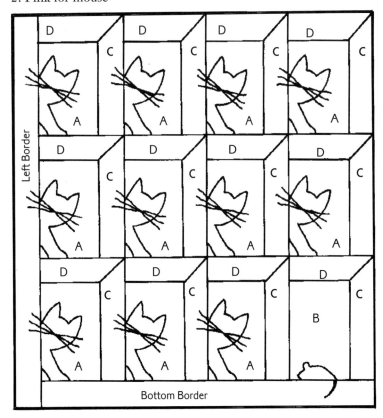

Assembly diagram

28

Printing Instructions

Small pieces of fabric are best not pinned to the print board; pins are not really needed, and they get in the way. However, because the piece is not secured to the print board, it may cling to the back of the screen after printing. To remove the print from the screen, turn the entire screen upside down and carefully peel the print off.

1. Print the background of the cat, using dark-blue ink, in the center of eleven of the 3 1/2- x 2 1/2-inch rectangles of print cloth.

2. Print the background of the mouse, using dark-blue ink, in the center of the twelfth 3 1/2- x 2 1/2-inch rectangle of print cloth.

3. Using pink ink, print the mouse after the blue background has dried. Take care in placing this stencil so the pink mouse completely fills the space left in the background.

Assembly Instructions

1. Sew the printed squares, sashings, and borders together in the conventional manner.

2. Next, attach the mouse's tail and the cats' whiskers. Make the mouse's tail by knotting the end of a short length of the embroidery floss and pulling it through from the back of the quilt top at the mouse's rump. Cut to an appropriate length (about 3/4 inch): then put a drop of glue or Fray Check at the end of the tail.

Use black quilting thread for the cats' whiskers, attaching them in the center of the face and also at the ends of the whiskers.

3. Layer the quilt top, batting, and backing; then baste the layers together.

4. Quilt as desired and bind with the dark-blue strips.

Full-size pattern for cutting sashing strip C

Full-size pattern for cutting sashing strip D

A. Full-size pattern for the cat background. Solid lines are stencil cutting lines and broken lines are seam lines

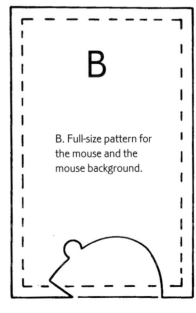

B. Full-size pattern for the mouse and the mouse background.

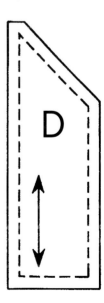

BROKEN HEXAGONS

A wall hanging that combines screen printing and patchwork

(overall size: 36 x 56 inches).

(Equilateral triangles are the building blocks of hexagons—six triangles make a hexagon.)

Stencils Required

Only one stencil is needed, and it is very easy to cut. Because all the lines are straight, a metal-edge ruler can be used as a guide for cutting. The stencil is composed of numerous stripes with open spaces between the stripes, so it will work much better with cut-lacquer film than with plastic or paper. You will clean the stencil between colors and use it to print all the different-colored triangles from which the hexagons are assembled.

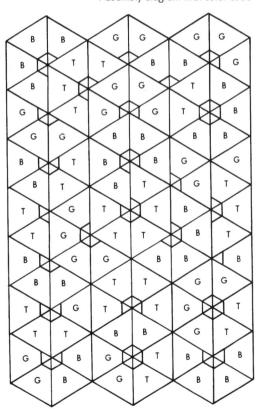

Assembly diagram with color code

(The small triangles in the diagram show the positioning of the stencil tips)

Ink Colors

1. Blue (B)
2. Green (G)
3. Turquoise, or blue-green (T)

Fabric Required

1. Print cloth: 2 yards.
2. Backing fabric: 2 yards in your choice of color. Suggestions are white, light blue, or light green.

Cutting Instructions

1. From the print cloth, cut 90 equilateral triangles (each side will measure 7 1/2 inches), plus a few extra for practice printing. The fabric triangle is 1/4 inch larger all around than the stencil to allow for some latitude in placing it for printing. (You can use the stencil pattern to make a pattern for cutting your triangles; just add 1/4 inch to all three sides.)
2. Cut the backing fabric into a piece that measures approximately 38 by 58 inches.

Printing Instructions

Remember to wash and thoroughly dry the stencil and frame after each color change.
1. Print 33 blue (B) triangles.
2. Print 29 green (G) triangles.
3. Print 28 turquoise (T) triangles.
4. Heat-set the 90 triangles (see page 25).
5. Carefully trim the excess fabric at the outer edges of each print.

Assembly Instructions

Piece the quilt top according to the assembly diagram at left. Baste quilt top, batting, and backing together. Quilt as desired, but do not quilt closer than 1 inch from the outside edges to allow for a neat edge finish, which is accomplished as follows:

1. Trim batting and backing to the same size as the quilt top.
2. Trim away the seam allowance of the batting only.
3. Turn under the seam allowance of the quilt top and baste with the edge of the batting enclosed inside.
4. Turn under the seam allowance of the backing so the edges of the top and backing are even.
5. Slip-stitch the two edges together.
6. Complete the quilting around the edges of the quilt.

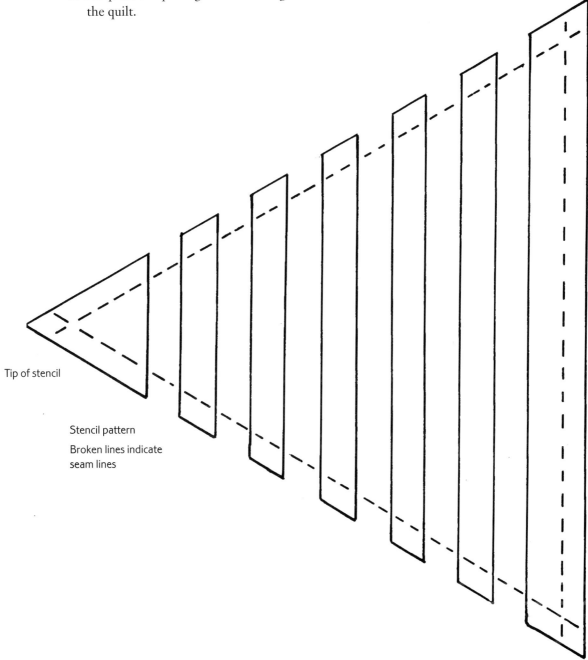

Tip of stencil

Stencil pattern

Broken lines indicate seam lines

PHIL O'DENDRON

An easy-to-print, full-size quilt

(overall size: 90 inches square)

This leafy, green quilt consists of 225 printed squares that combine two shades of green with white.

Stencils Required

1. Philodendron leaf (positive image)
2. Background around the philodendron leaf (negative image)
3. Entire square (for colored squares with no image)

All three stencils are prepared from a single stencil pattern. Although both paper and plastic can be used to make the stencil, plastic will be more durable for the many prints you will make. Cut the leaf part of the stencil for the negative image slightly smaller than you cut the leaf part for the positive image; this is because on some squares, you will use both the positive and negative images and they should overlap (no gaps between them).

Ink Colors

1. Light green
2. Dark green

Fabric Required

1. Print cloth (white): 7 1/2 yards for the quilt top
2. Print cloth (white) for a double binding: approximately 1/2 yard.
3. Backing fabric: 7 3/4 yards (A light-green solid or print would be appropriate.)

Cutting Instructions

1. Cut print cloth into 225 blocks, each 7 inches square (cut a few extra for printing practice).
2. Using the 1/2 yard of print cloth, cut ten 2-inch wide crosswise strips for the binding.

Printing Instructions

The quilt top is made of blocks ar-ranged in concentric squares around a central dark-green square. Consult the assembly diagram and the table below to see how many blocks of each color you will need.

1. Print each 7-inch block in the colors and quantities indicated in the table (note that

Square	# of Blocks	Leaf Color	Background Color
1	56	White (quilted only)	White
2	48	Light green	White
3	40	Dark green	White
4	32	White	Light green
5	24	Dark green	Light green
6	16	White	Dark green
7	8	Light green	Dark green
8	1	Dark green	Dark green (quilted only)

there are fifty-six white blocks and one dark-green block with no printing at all).
2. Heat-set all prints (see page 25).
3. Trim each block to 6 1/2 inches square.

Assembly diagram

32

Assembly Instructions

If you quilt on a frame, assemble the entire quilt top. Add batting and backing layers, baste together and quilt, incorporating the leaf motif into the unstenciled squares. Add binding.

If you lap quilt, as I do, you may assemble nine-block segments for quilting. Add batting and backing to each segment, baste layers together, and quilt each segment separately. When all segments are quilted, place the edges of two segments together and match all small block seams. Sew through only the quilt face, not the batting or backing. Turn the two joined segments face down and smooth the seam flat. Trim excess batting so the edges meet but do not overlap. Turn one edge of the backing under 1/4 inch and lap it over the remaining edge. Slipstitch the seam. Join all segments in this manner. Add binding.

Stencil Pattern
Broken line indicates seam line

A crib quilt constructed of blocks and sashing

(overall size: 38 x 39 inches)

One of the best features of the design is that this quilt looks good in almost any pair of colors you choose.

Stencils Required

1. Kitten stencil can be made of plastic or paper since it is a simple silhouette.
2. Single-heart stencil can also be made of paper or plastic and is used for corners.
3. The three-hearts stencil is suggested as a convenience. It prints three hearts in a vertical row all at one time and can be made of paper or plastic.
4. For paper-doll stencil, use cut-lacquer.

Ink Colors

Any two compatible colors

Fabric Required

1. Print cloth: about 1 1/4 yards for blocks and sashing.
2. Fabric for binding. (*Tip:* I often choose to make the binding from a fabric in one of the two colors I am going use in the quilt face. Buy this fabric first, and mix your printing ink to match it.)
3. Fabric for backing: about 1 1/4 yards. This can be print cloth or any compatible light-color solid or print.

Assembly diagram

34

Cutting Instructions

1. Cut print cloth as follows:

For paper doll blocks, nine 9- x 9 1/2-inch rectangles

For vertical sashing segments, twelve 3 1/2- x 8 7/8-inch strips

For horizontal sashing segments, twelve 3 1/2- x 8 7/8-inch strips.

For sashing corners, sixteen 3 1/2- x 3 1/2-inch squares.

2. For the binding, cut four 42- x 1 3/4-inch strips either of print cloth or other suitable fabric.

Printing Instructions

1. Print the paper dolls, five in one color and four in the other.
2. Using the kitten stencil, print 12 horizontal sashing strips.
3. Using the single-heart stencil, print 16 sashing corners.
4. Using the triple-heart stencil, print 12 vertical sashing strips.
5. When all prints are dry, heat-set them according to instructions on page 25.
6. Trim block to measure 8 7/8" square.

Assembly Instructions

1. Sew the quilt-top pieces together as indicated in the assembly diagram.
2. Baste quilt top, batting, and backing together.
3. Quilt as desired.
4. Bind the quilt.

Dotted line indicates center of design (for boy & girl shapes)

Broken line is seam line

A medallion-type wall quilt using autumn colors

(overall size: 40 inches square)

Bare trees in winter have strong features, and I have several quilt designs utilizing their compelling silhouette. As it happens, the logo for our nationally known Kentuck Festival of the Arts is also a tree, and it was for that event that this quilt was made.

The cutting of the pieces for the border is the most time-consuming part of this project, but I think you'll agree that the bor-

der is so distinctive it merits the time it takes. As a matter of fact, you may find this border to be the perfect accent for other quilts.

Stencils Required

1. The autumn leaf is easy to cut because all lines are straight. The two sets of outside lines, one broken and one solid, represent the placement of the leaf stencil on the fabric pieces A and B. You may want to make a separate stencil for A and B.

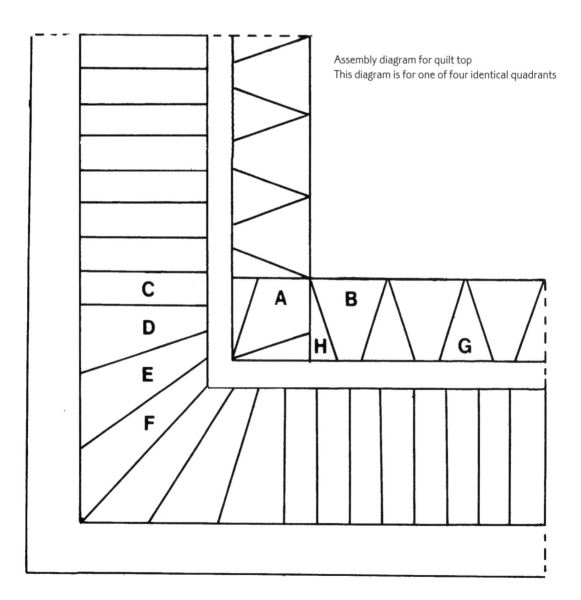

Assembly diagram for quilt top
This diagram is for one of four identical quadrants

2. The large tree is made using the stencil patterns for the four quadrants, all of which are different. The broken lines indicate where the design is to be joined. Although the tree involves free-hand cutting, the nature of the design is such that strict adherence to it is hardly necessary. Almost anything you cut will be satisfactory. Because both the leaf and the tree are silhouettes, loose plastic stencils will serve as well as those made using with cut-lacquer film.

Ink Colors

Dark green and rust brown. Mix to match your dark-green and rust-brown fabrics.

Fabrics Required

1. Print cloth in off-white: about 3/4 yard for center block and border pieces
2. Dark green: 3/4 yard
3. Rust brown: 5/8 yard
4. Gold: 3/8 yard
5. Light grayed-green: 3/8 yard
6. Medium grayed-green: 3/8 yard
7. Fabric for backing and binding: about 1 1/2 yards. This can be any of the colors listed above, or another compatible fabric.

Cutting Instructions

1. For printing the tree, cut an 18 1/2-inch square of off-white print cloth.
2. For leaves (inside border), cut as follows:
Pattern A: 4 pieces in medium grayed-green.
Pattern B: 8 pieces in medium grayed-green and 16 in light grayed-green.
Pattern G: 20 in gold.
Pattern H: 16 in gold.
3. For outside striped border, cut as follows:
Pattern C: cut 11 pieces each of off-white, rust brown, dark green, and gold
10 pieces each of light grayed-green and medium grayed-green
Pattern D: cut 1 piece each of gold, dark green, off-white, and rust brown, 2 pieces each of light gray-green and medium gray-green.

Pattern E: cut 1 piece each of dark green, gold, rust brown, and off-white, 2 pieces each of medium gray-green and light gray-green
Pattern F: cut 1 piece each of off-white, medium gray-green, light gray-green, and dark green, 2 pieces each of gold and rust brown
4. For the rust brown strip around the inside border: cut four strips measuring 1 1/2 x 26 1/2 inches. (This length allows for mitered corners.)
5. For the rust brown strip around the outside border, cut four strips 2 1/4 x 40 inches. (Also allows for mitered corners.)
6. For the binding (which I always prefer to be a double thickness), cut dark-green strips 1 3/4 inches wide for a total length of about 165 inches.

Printing Instructions

This larger design will require a printing frame at least 20 inches square and a squeegee about 16 inches wide.
1. Print the tree using rust-brown ink on the large off-white square of print cloth.
2. Print a dark-green leaf on each piece of fabric cut with Pattern A.
3. Print a dark-green leaf on each piece of fabric cut with Pattern B.
4. To produce the "spot of color" effect seen in the background, simply crumple the area to be spotted and dab it into different colors of wet ink. A pane of glass serves nicely as a palette for the inks. Be sure the tree print is thoroughly dry before you spot the background with color.
5. Dry and heat-set all prints.

Assembly Instructions

Seam allowances throughout are 1/4 inch.
1. Assemble the pieces of the quilt top using the photograph on page 00; for the borders, refer to the assembly diagram.
2. Add batting and backing and baste the three layers together.
3. Complete all quilting.
4. Add the binding.

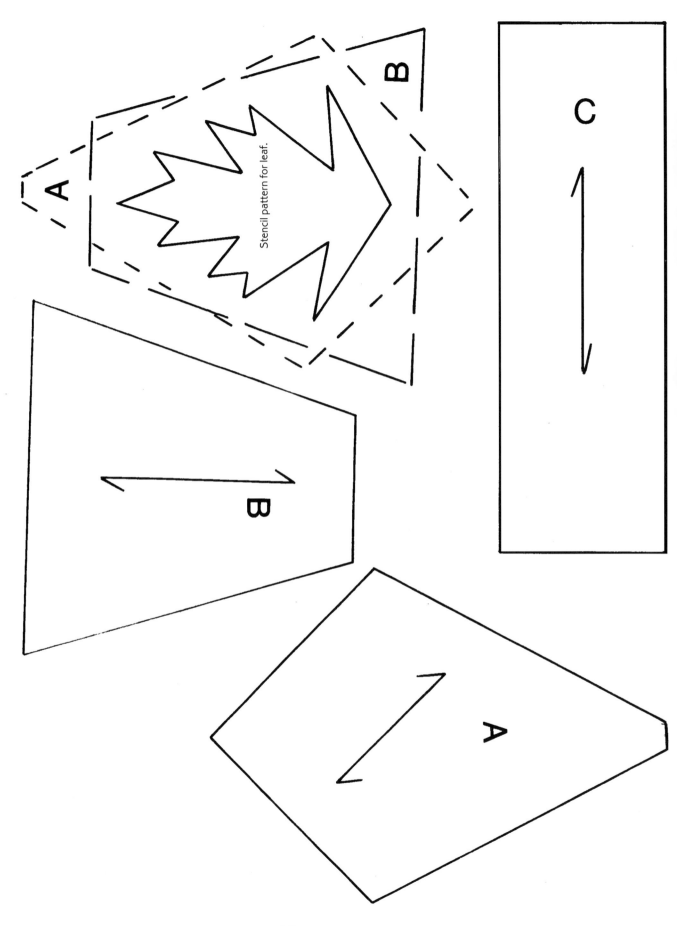

Stencil pattern for leaf.

A

B

C

B

A

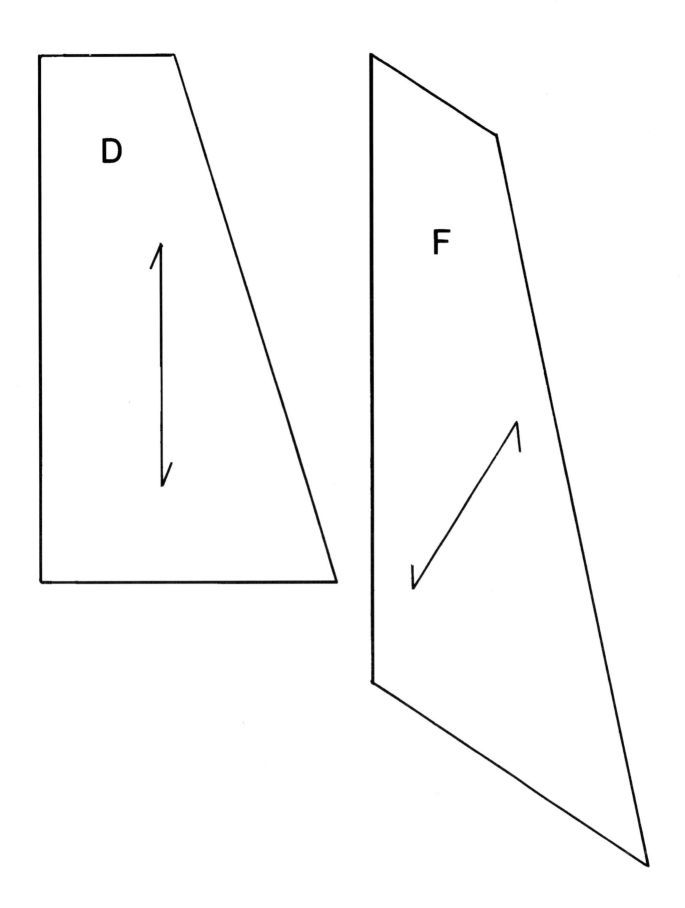

D

F

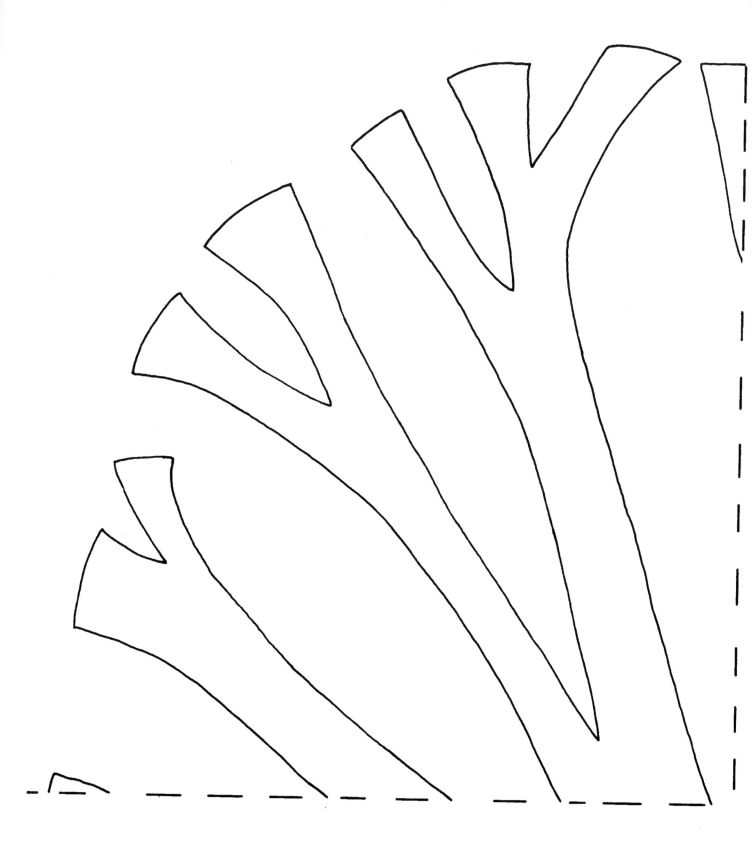

Stencil pattern for left top quadrant of tree

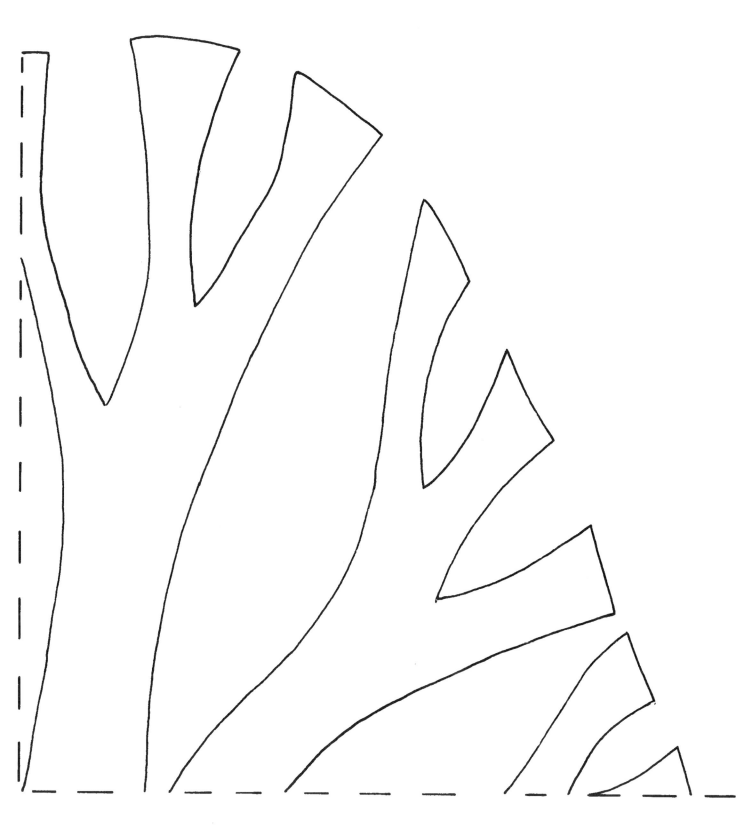

Stencil pattern for right top quadrant of tree

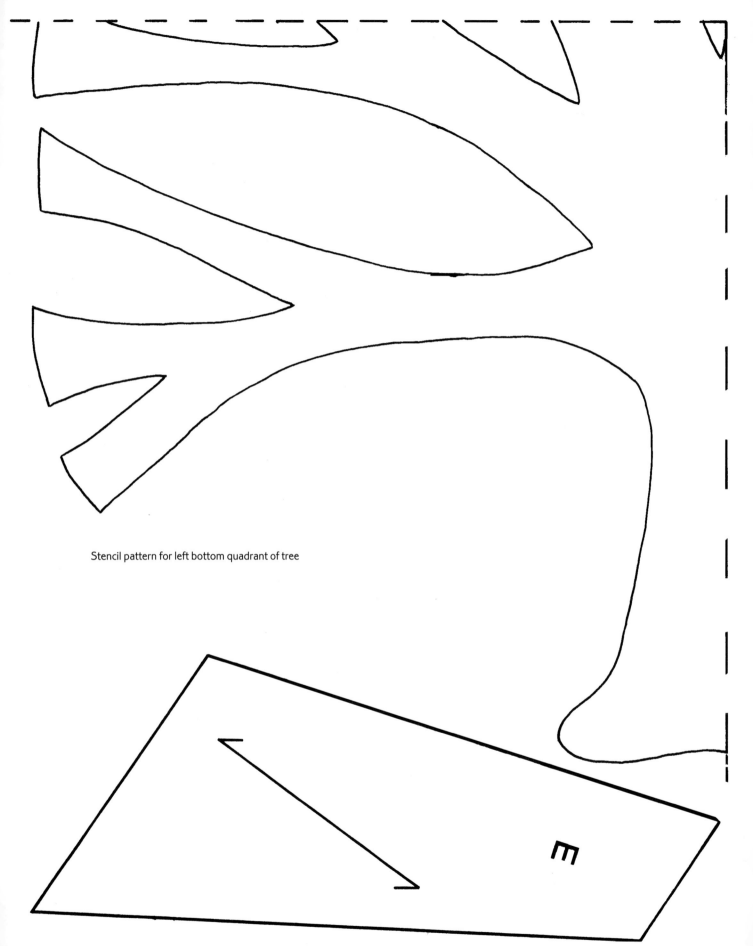

Stencil pattern for left bottom quadrant of tree

E

44

Stencil pattern for right bottom quadrant of tree

G

H

A repeated-stencil wall quilt

(overall size: 43 inches square)

This quilt calls for taking three diamonds in different sizes and colors and printing all of them on one stretch of fabric. The good news is that you end up with no seams to quilt along or across. The bad news is that one single misprint means starting all over again with fresh fabric.

However, when you accomplish this level of printing skill, the world is pretty much wide open to you. You are only limited by your imagination and ability to cut stencils.

Stencils Required

1. Diamond with small (S) bands
2. Diamond with medium (M) bands
3. Diamond with large (L) bands.

These should be cut-lacquer stencils. Each is small and easy to cut because all lines are straight. You can use a metal ruler and an X-Acto knife.

Ink Colors

Brick, rust, and gold, are used in my example. The brick-colored ink was mixed to match the brick-colored fabric of the border, and rust-colored ink to match the rust-colored fabric of the binding. You may choose any three colors you desire.

Diamond Color	Symbol	Diamond Band	Symbol
Gold	G	Large	L
Rust	R	Medium	M
Brick	B	Small	S

Printing diagram

Fabrics Required

1. Print fabric, either white or off-white: 1 1/4 yards
2. Brick-colored fabric: 1/4 yard
3. Rust-colored fabric: 1/4 yard
4. Backing fabric: 1 1/4 yards in a compatible fabric

Cutting Instructions

1. Cut a 42-inch square of print cloth for the quilt top.
2. For the border, cut four 2 1/8- x 42-inch strips selvage to selvage from the brick-colored fabric.
3. For a double binding, cut five 1 3/4-x 45-inch strips selvage to selvage from the rust-colored fabric.
4. For the backing, use a 45-inch square of compatible fabric.

Printing Instructions

The Printing Diagram is coded so that each diamond can be printed in the proper place. The letter codes appear in the upper quadrant of each diamond. The keys to color and bar size appear below.

1. Stretch the 42-inch square of print cloth on a print board and pin it in place.
2. Mark horizontal and vertical positioning lines. Stretch black threads over the print cloth, anchoring them with T-pins to the edges of the print board (see page 24). If you make your positioning lines the same as the horizontal and vertical lines of the Printing Diagram, you will find them to be very helpful in this rather complicated project.

(*Note:* Do not print over these threads; they will leave a little white line. If one crosses an open part of the stencil after the printing frame is in place, carefully move it out of the way, without disturbing the frame.)

3. Print all diamonds of one color—gold, for example—using the L stencil. Wash the stencil and put it aside to dry. While the L stencil is drying, print all the gold diamonds using the M stencil. Wash that stencil and put it aside to dry. Now print all the gold diamonds with the S stencil.
4. For the second color—rust, perhaps—repeat the entire procedure using the L, M, and S stencils, washing and drying each stencil after use.
5. Repeat the process a third time, using ink of the third color, which, in this example, is brick.
6. After all of the diamonds have been printed and all have been blown dry, heat-set this part of the quilt top.

Assembly Instructions

1. Attach the border strips to the printed quilt top.
2. Add batting and backing and baste the three layers together.
3. Complete all quilting.
4. Add the binding.

Stencil pattern for small (S) band diamonds

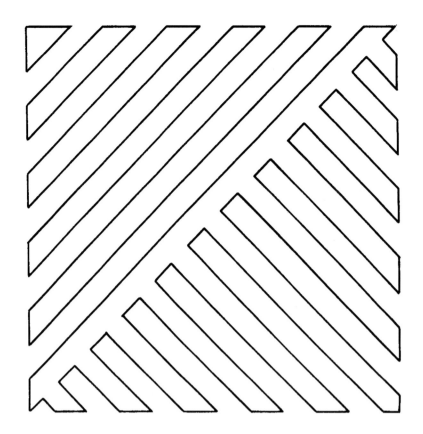

Stencil pattern for medium
(M) and diamonds

Stencil pattern for large (L)
band diamonds

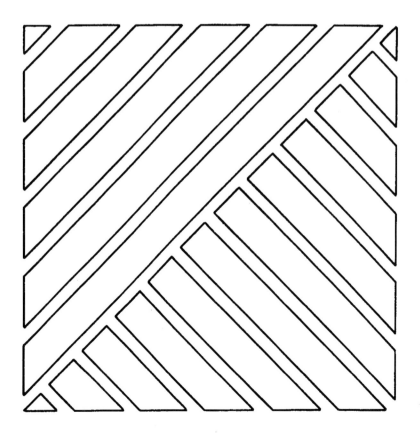

48

WHICH CAME FIRST?

A wall quilt with blocks and sashing

(overall size: 41 1/2 inches x 41 1/8 inches)

A visual pun on the age-old question gets us no closer to the answer, but this quilt design will brighten any area in your house. Try it as a crib quilt, or hang it on the wall in a child's room. And, of course, it would be marvelous in your kitchen.

Stencils Required

Use cut-lacquer film for all stencils.

1. For horizontal sashing, make one long stencil by combining Chicks A and Chicks B stencil patterns. Since you will print yellow chicks on a red background, you will need to cut two stencils, one with the background removed so you can print the red area and one with the chicks removed so you can print the yellow area.
2. For vertical sashing, use Chicks C stencil pattern to cut one stencil for the red background and another for the yellow chicks.
3. Brown sashing corner (contains four eggs, but since they are the white of the background, you only need one stencil with the background cut away.)
4. Main body of rooster
5. Main body of hen
6. Bill and legs of rooster
7. Bill and legs of hen
8. Comb and wattles of rooster
9. Comb and wattles of hen
10. Small circle stencil (use for brown inner eye of rooster and hen and for chick eyes)

Ink Colors

1. Brown
2. Red
3. Yellow

There are other color possibilities. You might think of printing this quilt in three shades of blue for an unusual effect.

Fabric Required

1. Print cloth: 1 1/2 yards. You may wish to use an off-white or ecru cotton or unbleached muslin, but test it first to see if the printing ink bleeds.
2. Print cloth for borders and binding: about 1/2 yard. (As an alternative, you may prefer to buy 1/4 yard of red fabric for the binding. If so, you must match your printing ink to it.)
3. Backing fabric, 1 1/2 yards, compatible with quilt top.

Assembly diagram

49

Cutting Instructions

1. From the l 1/2 yards of print cloth, cut the following:
twelve 4-inch squares for the sashing corners
nine 4- x 8 1/2-inch strips for vertical sashing
eight 4- x 14 1/2-inch strips for horizontal sashing
six 9-x 15-inch rectangles for blocks. A practice block or two would be a good idea for this detailed project.
2. From the 1/2 yard of print cloth, cut:
four 1 3/4- x 43-inch strips for the binding.
four 2- x 42 1/2-inch strips for the border.

Printing Instructions

Before beginning any printing, consult the quilt photograph on page 20 and the Assembly Diagram. Placing stencils in the proper position is the most difficult part of this design because of very small, even tiny, areas of color. Although black positioning threads might be of some help, here's a better idea: look closely through each stencil to what is below it on the print board before you print; carefully align the new stencil; then print.

1. Print the red background on all horizontal sashing strips.
When dry, trim to 3 3/4 x 13 inches.
2. Print the yellow chicks on the horizontal sashing strips.
3. Print the red background in all vertical sashing strips.
When dry, trim to 3 3/4 x 8 1/8 inches.
4. Print the yellow chicks on the vertical sashing strips.
5. Print the 12 sashing squares (corners), using brown ink.
When dry, trim to 3 3/4 inches square.
6. Use brown ink to print the main body of the rooster and the hen on each of the 9- x 15-inch blocks. Let dry.
7. Using red ink, print the comb and wattles of the rooster and hen on each rectangular block. Let dry.
8. Print the bill and legs of the rooster and hen with yellow ink on each of the rectangular blocks.

50

Details for rooster

When dry, trim the blocks to 8 1/8-x 14 inches.

9. Print the brown chick eyes and the brown inner eyes of the rooster and hen as needed.

10. After all prints are dry, heat-set them.

Assembly Instructions

1. Assemble the printed pieces according to the Assembly Diagram on page 49.
2. Sew the border in place.
3. Add batting and backing and baste together.
4. Quilt as desired.
5. Add binding.

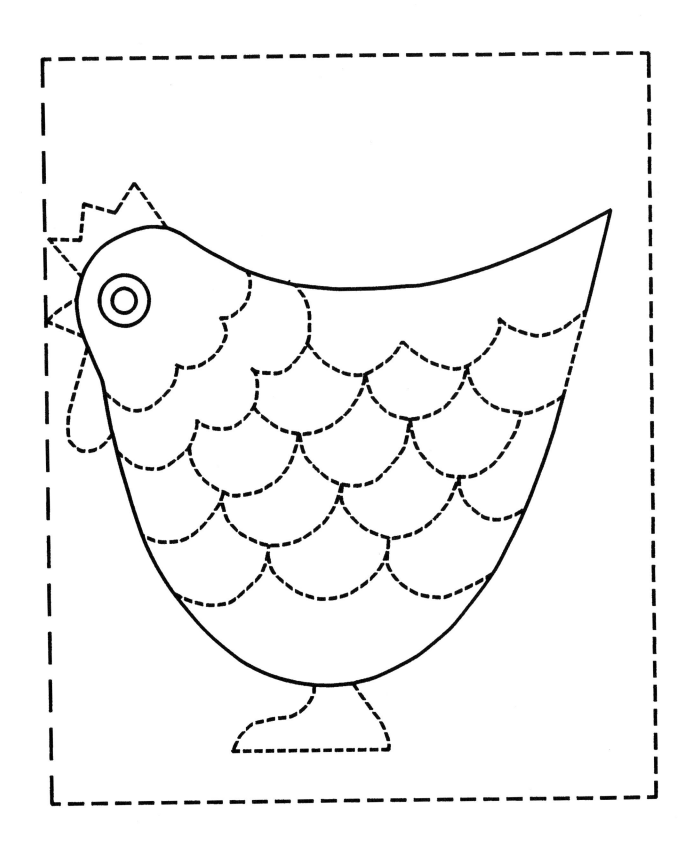

53

C

Details for hen

A hexagonal wall quilt

(overall size: approximately 43 inches across)

I said earlier that I really like working with equilateral triangles, and this quilt proves it. This large hexagon is made up of 216 small triangles, all the same size, but printed in different patterns and colors.

Stencils Required

Six different triangles are used; two of them require two colors, so the total number of stencils needed is eight. The stencils are not difficult to cut because all are straight lines, allowing you to use a metal ruler and an X-Acto knife. Cut-lacquer stencils are a must.

Ink Colors

1. Gold
2. Peach
3. Maroon
4. Medium brown
5. Dark brown to match binding.

Fabrics Required

1. Print cloth, either white or off-white: 1 7/8 yards
2. Medium-brown fabric for binding: 1/4 yard
3. Backing fabric: 1 1/8 yards

Cutting Instructions

1. Cut 216 equilateral triangles, each side 4 3/4 inches, from the print cloth. (Use one of the stencil patterns as a guide.)
2. From the medium-brown binding fabric, cut strips 1 3/4 inches wide totaling 130 inches in length.

Printing Instructions

Print the 216 triangles using the following code:

Triangle Pattern	Colors	Quantity
A. Narrow stripes	1. Medium brown on off-white	12
B. Wide stripes	2. Medium brown on off-white	36
C. Light half-diamonds	3. Off-white on dark brown	36
	4. Off-white on peach	6
D. Dark half-diamonds	5. Maroon on off-white	36
	6. Gold on off-white	6
E. Internal triangle	7. Dark brown inside medium brown	24
	8. Gold inside medium brown	12
	9. Peach inside maroon	12
F. Internal triangles	10. Maroon inside gold	12
	11. Medium brown inside peach	12
	12. Dark brown inside medium brown	12

Dry and heat-set all printed triangles. Carefully trim each so the pattern is straight and all sides measure 4 3/8 inches.

Assembly diagram for one sixth of the quilt top

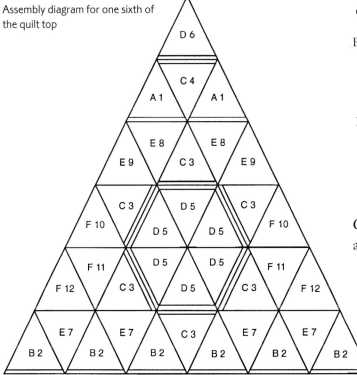

Assembly Instructions

1. Select the printed triangles required for one-sixth of the quilt top by reading the Assembly Diagram on page 55. The top is made from six identical segments; sort the printed triangles into six stacks of 36 triangles each.

2. Follow the Assembly Diagram to determine where each type of triangle belongs. Letters refer to patterns; numbers refer to colors (refer to the code in Printing Instructions if necessary). Note that some triangles are symmetrical (those coded E and F) and can be oriented in any direction in the quilt. Others (coded A, B, C and D) have a base and must be oriented in a particular direction, indicated in the Assembly Diagram. Sew triangles together in pairs, then in fours, and so on until all 36 are sewn together.

When the first segment is done, set it aside while completing five other identical segments.

3. Sew the six segments together to make the quilt top.

4. Add batting and backing; baste layers together.

5. Quilt as desired, by hand or machine.

6. Finish the edges with binding.

Broken line indicates trim line for printed triangles

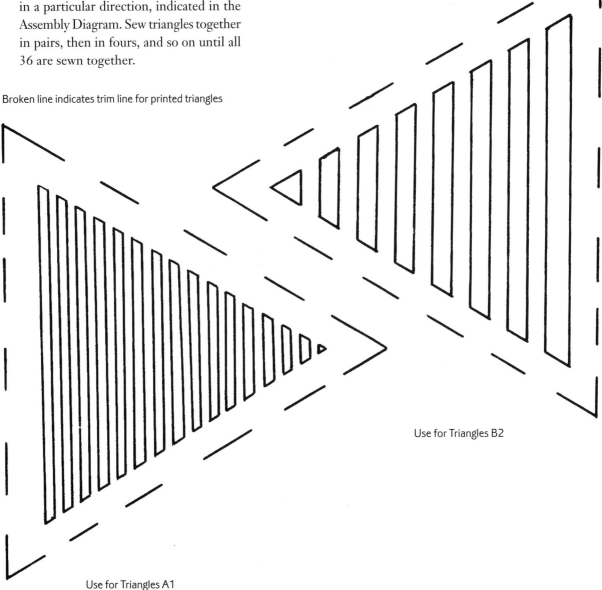

Use for Triangles B2

Use for Triangles A1

56

Use for Triangles E7, E8 and E9.
Cut and remove segments labeled o.

Use for Triangles E7, E8 and E9.
Cut and remove segments labeled o.

Use for Triangles F10, F11 and
F12. Cut and remove segments
labeled o

REACH OUT AND TOUCH SOMEONE

A wall quilt combining screen printing with appliquéd accents

(Overall size: 43 inches square)

This quilt symbolizes all human races living together in peace. For fun, the hands are embellished with bracelets, rings and painted fingernails. The message of the quilt seems to strike a chord with many folks, and they are charmed by the appliquéd accents. You will have as much fun deciding on the "jewelry" for the hands as I did.

Stencils Required

Only one stencil is needed. It may be of paper, plastic, or cut-lacquer.

Ink Colors

1. Pink (P)
2. Grayed yellow (Y)
3. Red-brown (R)
4. Medium brown (T)

5. Dark brown (B).

Fabric Required

1. For the quilt top: 1 1/4 yards of print cloth
2. For the binding: 1/4 yard of print cloth
3. For backing: 1 1/4 yards of white or other light-color fabric

Cutting Instructions

1. Cut the quilt top from print cloth to measure 43 inches square.
2. From the 1/4 yard of print cloth, cut four 1 3/4-inch wide strips selvage to selvage for the binding.
3. Cut a 43-inch square from the backing fabric.

Printing Instructions

This small quilt is not difficult to print because it uses only one stencil and one large piece of fabric. Consult the printing diagram and the color code before beginning to print; this will help you familiarize yourself with the arrangement and color placement of the hands.

The quilt top contains 10 dark-brown hands, 9 red-brown hands, 10 medium-brown ones, 11 yellow, and 10 pink.

Stretch the print cloth on a print board and pin it in place. Indicate horizontal and vertical reference lines on the print cloth, using stretched black threads pinned to the printing board (see page 24). The grid lines on the printing diagram show where these threads should be located. Be certain that you do not ink over the positioning threads because you will have white lines on your print.

Assembly diagram

59

Print all the hands of one color; then wash and dry the screen and print the hands of the second color. Repeat this procedure for the hands of the third, fourth, and fifth colors.

After each hand has been printed, dry it with a blow-dryer. When all printing is completed, heat-set the quilt top. (See page 25.)

Embellishing the Quilt

Use your imagination to embellish the hands with appliquéd rings, bracelets, and painted fingernails.

Assembly Instructions

1. Add batting and backing to the quilt top and baste together.
2. Quilt as desired. Suggested for the outer white areas of the design are the words "Reach Out," for which a pattern is included.
3. Finish with binding.

Stencil pattern for hand

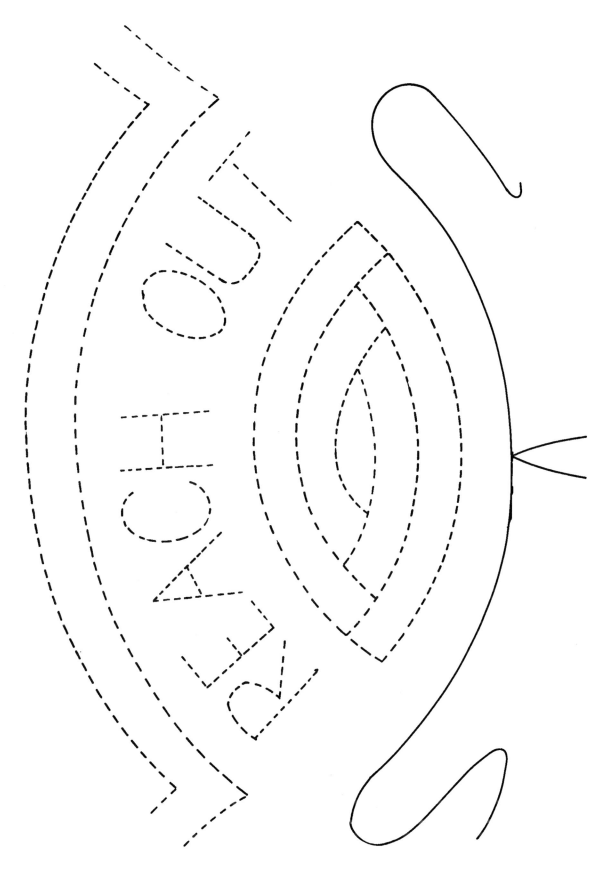

Quilting pattern

Quilting pattern

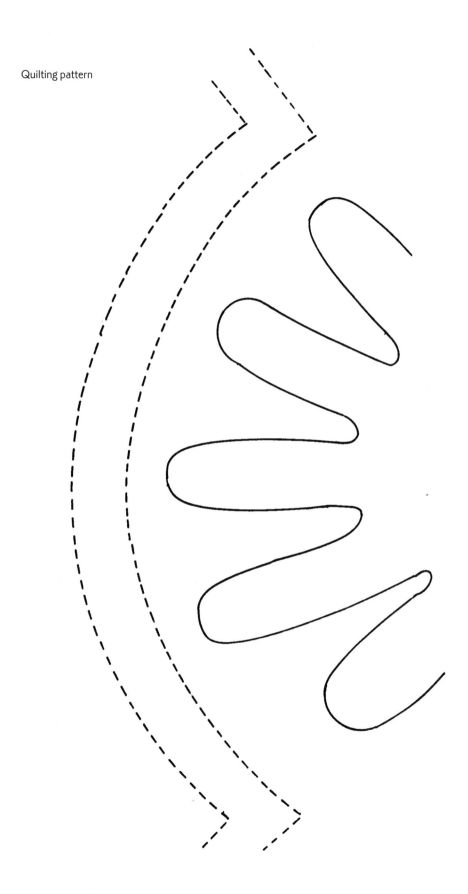

AFTER THE SUNSET

A wall quilt printed on a single piece of fabric

(overall size: 40 inches square)

The afterglow of a sunset over water was the inspiration for this quilt, as well as the reason for the blue diagonal that runs through the center of the design. Which is real and which is the reflection? On beautiful clear summer evenings, it is sometimes hard to tell.

Stencils Required

A single cut-lacquer stencil is used. Careful cutting is required to produce a good free-hand circle so use a circle-cutter if one is available. All of the lines within the circle utilize a straight-edge for cutting.

Ink Colors

1. Yellow
2. Yellow-orange
3. Orange
4. Red-orange
5. Red
6. Blue, in six tints, ranging from a very light sky blue to dark blue

Fabrics Required

1. Print cloth: 1 1/4 yards
2. Light-blue fabric: 3/8 yard
3. Medium-blue fabric: 1/4 yard
4. Backing fabric of your choice: 1 1/4 yards

Cutting Instructions

1. For the quilt top: cut a 40-inch square of print cloth.
2. Border: cut four 2 3/4 x 43-inch strips of light blue fabric.
3. Binding: cut four 1 3/4 x 43-inch strips of medium blue fabric.
4. Backing: cut a 44-inch square.

Printing Instructions

Consult the two Printing Diagrams before beginning to print. The diagrams and the table are labeled so that each circle can be printed in its proper place.

Circle Color	Code
Yellow	Y
Yellow-orange	YO
Orange	O
Red-orange	RO
Red	R
Very light blue	B1
Light blue	B2
Sky blue	B3
Blue	B4
Royal blue	B5
Dark blue	B6

1. Stretch the 40-inch square of print cloth on a print board and pin it in place. To position the stencils on the cloth, use horizontal reference lines (stretched and pinned black thread, see page 24).
2. Study the color photo on page 22 to determine proper placement of the stencil. Then, starting at the upper left corner of your print cloth, print the row of eleven odd-numbered circles from left to right. Be sure to blow dry each circle as soon as it is printed. The left side of the circle being printed should just touch the right side of the previously printed (and blown-dry) circle. Notice that the stripes within these circles are oriented vertically.
3. Now print the even-numbered circles; these are positioned midway between the odd-numbered ones (again, study the color photo). The stripes within these circles are oriented horizontally. Blow-dry each circle as soon as it is printed. You will soon notice that where circles overlap, a plaid pattern results and new colors appear. For example, overlapping yellow and blue circles produce a green plaid.

4. After all of the circles have been printed and are thoroughly dry, heat-set the entire printed surface.

   Note: The stencil used here is also used in the bed-sized quilt *Spheres of Influence* shown on the cover of this book. If you want to make a full-size quilt like *Spheres of Influence*, you will need five additional stencils:
   1. 3-inch circle stencil with narrow bands
   2. 3-inch circle stencil with wide bands
   3. 6-inch circle stencil with narrow bands
   4. 6-inch circle stencil with medium bands
   5. 6-inch circle stencil with wide bands

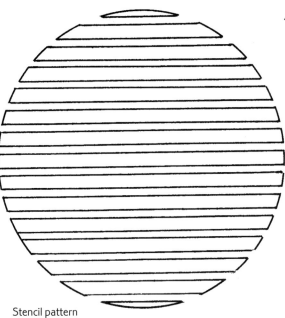

Stencil pattern

Make yourself Printing Diagrams for your bed-size quilt similar to the example given for this project; first, you must decide how large you want the finished quilt to be. Then, you will figure how many printed circles, both horizontally and vertically, it will take to fill the space.

Assembly Instructions

1. Attach border strips to the printed square.
2. Make a sandwich of the quilt top, batting, and backing; baste together.
3. Quilt as desired (I recommend quilting around each of the circles).
4. Bind the quilt.

1	3	5	7	9	11	13	15	17	19	21
Y	Y	Y	Y	Y	Y	Y	Y	Y	Y	B6
Y	Y	Y	Y	Y	Y	Y	Y	Y	B6	B6
YO	YO	YO	YO	YO	YO	YO	YO	B5	B5	B5
YO	YO	YO	YO	YO	YO	YO	B5	B5	B5	B5
O	O	O	O	O	O	B5	B5	B5	B5	B5
O	O	O	O	O	B4	B4	B4	B4	B4	B4
RO	RO	RO	RO	B4	B4	B4	B4	B4	B4	B4
RO	RO	RO	B3	B3	B3	B3	B3	B3	B3	B3
R	R	B3	B3	B3	B3	B3	B3	B3	B3	B3
B2	B2	B2	B2	B2	B2	B2	B2	B2	B2	B2
B1	B1	B1	B1	B1	B1	B1	B1	B1	B1	B1

Printing diagram for odd-numbered rows of circles

2	4	6	8	10	12	14	16	18	20
B1	B1	B1	B1	B1	B1	B1	B1	B1	B1
B2	B2	B2	B2	B2	B2	B2	B2	B2	Y
B3	B3	B3	B3	B3	B3	B3	B3	Y	YO
B3	B3	B3	B3	B3	B3	B3	Y	YO	YO
B4	B4	B4	B4	B4	B4	Y	YO	YO	O
B4	B4	B4	B4	B4	Y	YO	YO	O	O
B5	B5	B5	B5	Y	YO	YO	O	O	RO
B5	B5	B5	Y	YO	YO	O	O	RO	RO
B6	B6	Y	YO	YO	O	O	RO	RO	R
B6	Y	YO	YO	O	O	RO	RO	R	R
Y	YO	YO	O	O	RO	RO	R	R	R

Printing diagram for even-numbered rows

64

GRANDPA'S FARM

A crib quilt printed on a single piece of fabric

(Overall dimensions: 39 x 43 inches)

I sent this screen-printed quilt to a prestigious national show with no intention of trying to mislead anyone about its method of construction. Not only did the judges award it a ribbon, but one judge remarked that the appliqué was unusually neat.

Stencils Required

A. Trace the stencil pattern for the left side of the barn; turn the tracing over to get the stencil pattern for the right side. Cut stencil from paper, plastic, or cut-lacquer.

B. Barn cupola.

C. Cow: Make a cut-lacquer stencil. (Note that in my quilt, the four cows are identical except for their spots. If you want this variety, you need four different cut-lacquer stencils.) Use paper or plastic stencils to print the yellow spots on the red cows. Make the "spot" stencils slightly larger than the "holes" in the cow so the yellow will overlap the red slightly with no gapping.

D. Goose: One stencil pattern is provided. Turn this over to provide the mirror-image stencil pattern needed. Cut stencil from paper, plastic or cut-lacquer.

E. Pig: This stencil can be made of paper, plastic, or cut-lacquer.

F. Rooster, hen and chicks: Paper, plastic, or cut-lacquer stencils may be used. Turn the stencil patterns over to obtain the same figures in mirror images.

G. Horse: Prepare a wide cut-lacquer stencil, about 38 inches across and about 14 inches deep, for the sky; position the four white horses as shown in the Printing Diagram. (The horses are "floating centers.")

H. Sheep: prepare a large cut-lacquer stencil, in a roughly circular shape, about 14 X 18 inches, for the green pasture and place the sheep inside as "floating centers." To get the right shape, refer to the Printing Diagram, and enlarge the pasture about five times.

I. Green fence around pigs: Make a large cut-lacquer stencil about 15 inches across and 17 inches long, in an oval shape as shown in the Printing Diagram. The fence, which is about 1 inch wide, is a "floating center," and will look very much like a halo in the stencil.

Printing diagram for placement

65

J. Green fence under horses and around cows: Use a large piece of cut-lacquer to make this stencil, about 24 inches deep and about 38 inches across. It must match exactly the bottom of the print from the horse stencil. Cut the fences about 1 inch wide, as shown in the Printing Diagram. (You may enlarge the Printing Diagram five times if you wish to make a pattern for the fence, rather than drawing it free-hand.)

Ink Colors

1. Red
2. Green
3. Medium or sky blue
4. Pink
5. Yellow
6. Light gray.

(Note: If you select red or green fabric for your border and binding, mix your red and green ink to match the fabric.)

Fabric Required

1. For quilt top: 1 1/4 yards of print cloth
2. For backing: a 40- x 44-inch rectangle of print cloth or other suitable light-colored fabric.
3. For border and binding: 1/2 yard of red or green fabric.

Printing Instructions

1. Stretch the large piece of print fabric on a printing board, and pin it in place. Consult the printing diagram to determine where each figure is to be placed. Use each stencil as indicated, being particularly careful with the long blue stencil and the green strip stencil.
2. When all printing is completed and ink is thoroughly dry, heat-set the printed piece (see page 25).

Assembly Instructions

1. Trim your finished print into a rectangle that measures 35 1/2 x 38 1/2 inches.
2. Cut two border strips that measure 39 1/2 x 2 1/2 inches and two others that measure 43 1/2 x 2 1/2 inches. (This allows enough fabric to miter the corners.)
3. Sew the borders to the quilt top, add batting, and backing; baste the layers together.
4. Quilt as desired, or study color photograph on page 22 for suggestions.
5. Finish with binding.

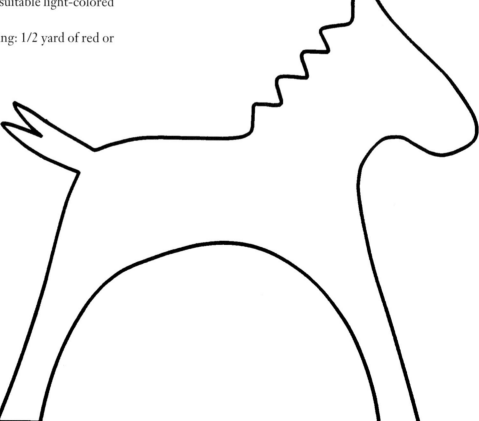

G. Horse

F. Rooster,
hen, and chicks

E. Pig

D. Goose

H. Sheep.

B. Cupola

67

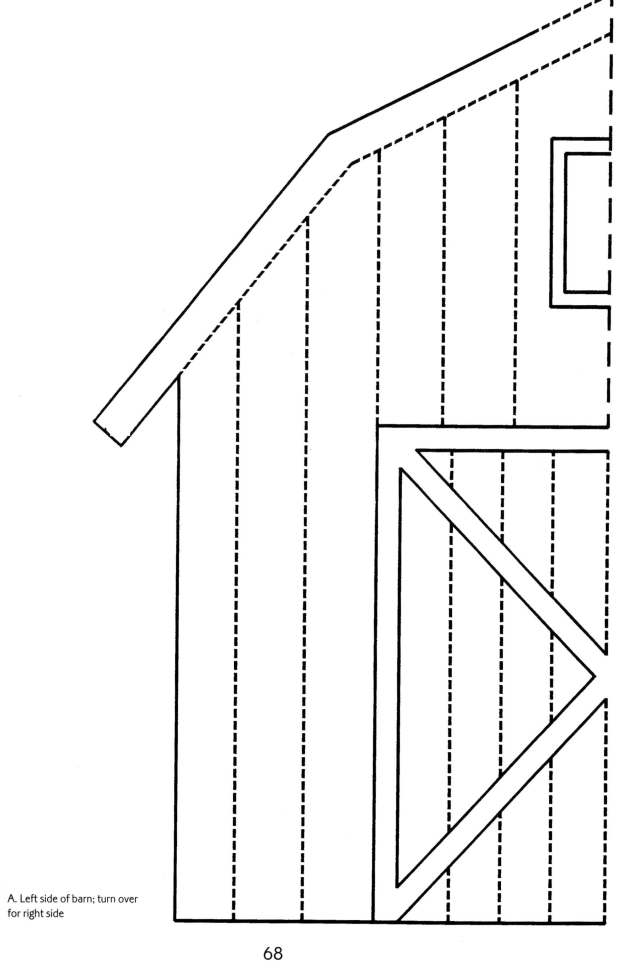

A. Left side of barn; turn over for right side

C. Cow

ZINNIAS IN THE WINDOWS OF MY LOG CABIN

A quilt combining the traditional log cabin style with screen printing

(Overall size: 75 x 83 inches)

Stencils Required

Although the quilt in the photograph on page 23 shows zinnias of different sizes, it is simpler and just as effective to use only one size of zinnia. With one flower size, you will need only three stencils, one for each different-colored layer of petals per flower. Since the petal layers are silhouettes, they can be plastic or paper stencils.

Ink Colors

Six colors are used for the zinnias; each color is printed in three values. The colors are lightened in two stages by adding extender or white. The colors are:

1. Yellow (Y)
2. Orange (O)
3. Red-orange (RO)
4. Red-violet (RV)
5. Pink (P)
6. Violet (V)

Fabrics Required

1. For printing the zinnias: 2 yards print cloth.
2. For "log" strips around zinnias and outer edge of quilt:

Dark grayed blue green (BD): 1 yard

Medium grayed blue green (BM): 1 yard

Light grayed blue green (BL): 1 yard

Dark green (GD): 1 yard

Medium green (GM): 7/8 yard

Light green (GL): 7/8 yard

Note: The "log" strips in the quilt shown in the photograph on page were hand-dyed, but commercially available fabric can be used. The important factor is that the fabrics must be available in dark, medium, and light shades of the two colors you choose.

3. For backing and binding: 2 1/2 yards of compatible fabric.

Cutting Instructions

1. Cut ninety 5 1/2-inch print cloth squares.
2. Cut all "log" strips 1 1/2 inches wide and in lengths indicated in the following cutting chart. This chart (plus the Assembly Diagrams) tells you where these strips belong in the quilt top.
3. Cut and piece backing material to make a rectangle that measures 75 x 83 inches. Cut binding strips on straight of grain 1 3/4 inches wide to equal approximately 320 inches in length.

Color and Assembly Code	Length of Strip (inches)	Number of Strips Required
BD1	8 1/2	54
BD2	7 1/2	45
BD5	9 1/2	1
BM1	8 1/2	8
BM2	7 1/2	45
BM3	6 1/2	45
BM5	9 1/2	1
BM6	10 1/2	1
BL1	8 1/2	8
BL3	6 1/2	45
BL4	5 1/2	45
BL6	10 1/2	1
BL71	1 1/2	1
GD1	8 1/2	54
GD2	7 1/2	45
GM1	8 1/2	9
GM2	7 1/2	45
GM3	6 1/2	45
GL1	8 1/2	9
GL3	6 1/2	45
GL4	5 1/2	4

Printing Instructions

When printing the zinnias, begin with the largest stencil, and use the lightest value of ink color. When the light ink dries, center the intermediate-sized stencil over the larger shape and print the medium value of the same color. Finally, center the smallest stencil over the two printed shapes and print the darkest value of the same color. Repeat this basic procedure until all the zinnias are printed.

Tip: It is more efficient to work with one color at a time. For example: Print all the 18 light-yellow zinnia forms; when dry, print the medium-yellow zinnia forms on the same squares; when dry, all the intense yellow centers on the same squares. Repeat for the other five colors.

Assembly Instructions

1. There are two Quilt Assembly Diagrams, A and B, to guide you in sewing the "logs" onto the printed squares. You will need 45 of Block A and 45 of Block B, a total of 90, for a full-sized quilt.

2. The A and B blocks are sewn together according to Diagrams C and F, with Diagram C indicating that the A and B blocks must be alternated, beginning at the upper left with an A block. Diagram F shows suggested color placement for the zinnias.

3. Before the quilt top can be finished, borders of logs on the bottom and right edges must be added. Diagrams D and E indicate the construction of these two borders. Begin at the bottom edge and sew the first pieced row to the quilt top. Then sew the first row to the side of the quilt top. Add the second row to the bottom, the second row to the side, and so on until finished. Although this sounds a bit cumbersome, it allows the corners to be interwoven properly.

4. With the top of the quilt completed, add batting and backing: baste together.

5. Quilt as desired, but do not quilt closer than 1 inch to the outside edges.

6. A knife-edge finish is appropriate and may be made by using the instructions on page 30-31.

Assembly diagram "F" showing arrangement of zinnia colors

P	V	O	Y	RV	O	V	RO	Y
RV	Y	RO	V	P	RV	Y	O	P
RO	O	P	Y	O	O	V	RV	RO
Y	P	V	O	Y	RV	RO	P	V
V	O	RV	RO	P	V	Y	O	RV
RV	Y	RO	P	RV	RO	P	V	Y
O	P	V	O	Y	P	RV	RO	O
P	RV	RO	P	RO	V	O	Y	R
RO	V	Y	RV	O	Y	P	RV	V
Y	O	P	RO	V	RV	RO	O	P

Assembly diagram "C" showing arrangement of "A" and "B" blocks

A	B	A	B	A	B	A	B	A
B	A	B	A	B	A	B	A	B
A	B	A	B	A	B	A	B	A
B	A	B	A	B	A	B	A	B
A	B	A	B	A	B	A	B	A
B	A	B	A	B	A	B	A	B
A	B	A	B	A	B	A	B	A
B	A	B	A	B	A	B	A	B
A	B	A	B	A	B	A	B	A
B	A	B	A	B	A	B	A	B

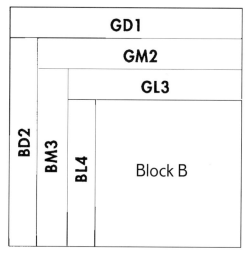

Assembly diagram for "A" blocks

Assembly diagram for "B" blocks

E. Assembly diagram for right edge

GL1 | GM1 | GD1 | BL1 | BM1 | BD1 | GL1 | GM1 | GD1 | BL1 | BM1 | BD1 | GL1 | GM1 | GD1 | BL1 | BM1 | BD1 | GL1 | GM1 | GD1 | BL7 | BM6 | BD5

D. Assembly diagram for lower border of quilt

BL1 | GL1 | BL1 | GL1 | BL1 | GL1 | BL1 | GL1 | GL1 | BL6
BM1 | GM1 | BM1 | GM1 | BM1 | GM1 | BM1 | GM1 | GM1 | BM5
BD1 | GD1 | BD1 | GD1 | BD1 | GD1 | BD1 | GD1 | GD1 | BD1

Stencil patterns for the zinnia

73

The designs in this section are included to inspire you, to show you what is possible with the marvelous technique of screen printing. If you have completed all the projects in this book, you will be accomplished enough to continue with screen printing, now with your original designs. You will also find it easy to adapt a pattern for almost any medium to a screen-printed quilt. The possibilities will soon exceed the time you have to devote to your craft.

Iowa Summer: 48 x 37 inches, 1985. I was raised on a farm in western Iowa, and revisited my home a few summers ago by way of a low-level flight. This quilt is my interpretation of that landscape. It was published in *Quilting Today* in 1992.

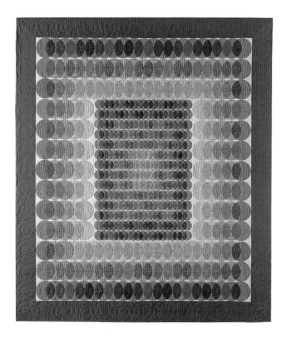

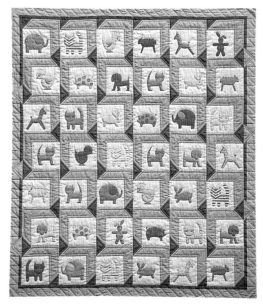

Spheres of Influence: 77 x 89 inches,1988. This quilt won a monetary award in the 1989 AQS quilt show in Paducah. One judge said it had a wonderful illusion of transparency. I gave it to our daughter, Celia. Photo courtesy of American Quilter's Society, Paducah, Ky. Photographer: Donahue Studios, Inc. Evansville, Tn.

Baby Blocks: 45 x 50 inches, 1991. This crib quilt was made to celebrate the birth of our first grandchild, Caitlin Moran, and given to her family soon after her arrival.

Hallie's Comet: 33 x 43 1/2 inches, 1985. This quilt was made the year of the return of Halley's Comet and included in a multimedia exhibit entitled **Images of the Universe: The Artist's Vision.** It was also shown the same year at the annual meeting of the American Society of Astronomers.

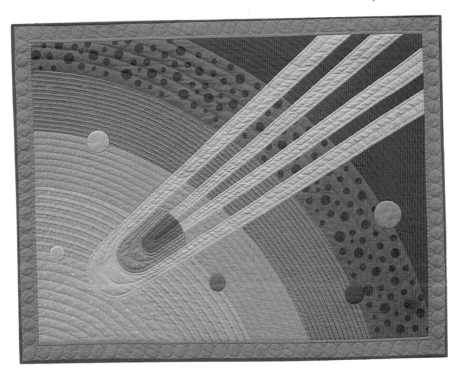

Just Fantastic: 72 x 94 inches, 1989. This quilt is on permanent loan to the Museum of the American Quilter's Society. Of course, I am enormously pleased to have it exhibited there. It took an Honorable Mention in the Theme category (which was "Fans") at the AQS show in 1990. It was published in *Quilting Today* in 1990. Photograph by Richard Walker.

Sunset at Tombeau Bay: 56 x 62 inches,1992. My husband, Charles, and I lived for a year at Tombeau Bay on the west side of the Island of Mauritius. Our favorite evening pastime was walking on the beach and viewing the tropical sunsets; this is my abstract interpretation of those pleasant times. Photograph courtesy of *McCall's Quilting;* it was published there in November 1993.

Accolade to Autumn: 75 1/2 x 85 inches, 1993. This quilt is a good example of how the familiar techniques of quiltmaking can be combined with screen printing. The multi-colored piecing in the area around the tree is intended to represent falling leaves. It won an Honorable Mention at the 1994 American Quilter's Society show in the Other Techniques category.

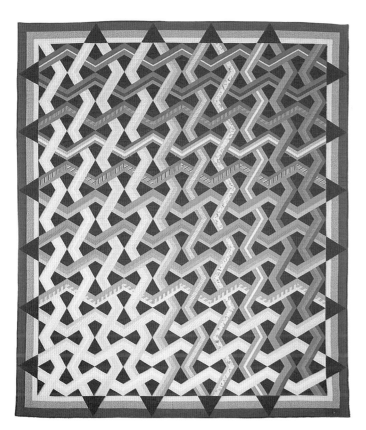

Kinetic Interlock: 81 x 94 inches, 1991. This active design began with a simple block which was reversed (mirror image) every other block. I chose colors that moved both horizontally and vertically across the quilt from yellow to blue.

Mollusca: 40 x 40 inches, 1984. The ocean was the inspiration for this quilt. The oscillating white line symbolizes wave action and the designs within these lines suggest sea shells. The colors were chosen because they are common to many shells.

Granddaughter's Flower Garden: 63 x 82 inches. A contemporary modification of an old favorite, "Grandmother's Flower Garden." This quilt won best-of-show award at the 14th annual Smoky Mountain Quilt Show.

List of Suppliers

Before contacting one of the companies listed, check the Yellow Pages in the metropolitan area nearest you. Look under "silk screen" or "screen printing" suppliers. Many of your needs can be supplied by local agents.

Craft Industries Limited
P. O. Box 38
Somerset, MA 02726-0038
(508)-676-3883

PROfab textile ink; Pebeo Setacolor inks
Pebeo Setacolor Transparent

Dharma Trading Co.
P. O. Box 150916
San Rafael, CA 94915

"Versatex" screen-printing ink, cotton print cloth, Deka Permanent Fabric Paint

Hunt Manufacturing Co.
Domestic Customer Service
P. O. Box 5830
Statesville, NC 28677
800-438-0977

Textile inks
printing accessories, such as squeegees and frame strips

The Naz-Dar Company
1087 North Branch Street
Chicago, IL 60622
(312) 943-8215

WAT-R-TEX screen printing inks, stencil materials, squeegees

PRO Chemical and Dye, Inc.
P. O. Box 14PRO
Somerset, MA 02726
(508)-676-3838

PROfab textile ink.

Sax Arts and Crafts
P. O. Box 2002
316 North Milwaukee Street
Milwaukee, WI 53201
800-558-6696

Colortex Textile pigments and base

Testfabrics, Inc.
P. O. Drawer 0
200 Blackford Avenue
Middlesex, NJ 08846

Cotton print cloth

Ulano
210 East 86th Street
New York, NY 10028

Stencil materials and stencil cutters

Union
453 Broad Avenue
Ridgefield, NJ 07652
800-526-0455

Unidye pigment (inks) opaque fabric

To Learn More

Auvil, Kenneth W. *Serigraphy: Silk Screen Techiques for the Artist.*
Englewood Cliffs, N.J.: Prentice Hall Inc., 1965

Banzhaf, Robert A. *Screen Process Printing.* Bloomington, Ill.:
McKnight Publishing Co., 1983. (Contains a chapter on printing on fabric.)

Bigeleisen, J. I. *Screen Printing.* New York: Watson-Guptil Publications, 1971.
(Contains a chapter on printing on fabric.)

Hollebone, Sarah. *Screen Printing: The Beginner's Guide.*
London: A. and C. Black,1980. (Contains a chapter on printing on fabric.)

Kinsey, Anthony. *Simple Screen Printing.*
Leicester, England or Woodridge, N.J.: The Dryad Press,1971.

Kosloff, Albert. *Mitography is Screen Printing.*
Chicago, Ill: Naz-Dar Company,1975.

Russ, Stephen. *Fabric Painting by Hand.*
New York: Watson-Guptil Publications, 1966. (A description of tools and materials for
printing on fabric by hand; contains a chapter on screen printing.)

Saff, Donald, and Deli Sacillotto. *Screen Printing: History and Process.*
New York: Rinehart and Winston, 1979. (Describes the historical development of screen
printing on fabric.)

Schwalback, Mathilda V., and James A. Schwalback. *Screen Process Printing for the
Serigrapher and Textile Designer.*
New York: Van Nostrand Reinhold Co., 1970.

Seazie, Valeria, and Roberta Clayson. *Screen Process Printing on Fabric.*
New York: Watson-Guptil Publications,1969. (A description of screen printing on
textiles, with suggestions for design motifs.)

Swerdlow, Robert M. *The Step-by-Step Guide to Screen-Process Printing.*
Englewood Cliffs, N.J.: Prentice-Hall, Inc., 1985. (An up-to-date description of the
general procedures involved in screen printing, including photographic techniques.)